THE ART OF READING

Damon Young is a prize-winning philosopher and writer. He is the author of seven books, including *How to Think About Exercise*, *Philosophy in the Garden*, and *Distraction*. His works are published internationally in English and translation, and he has also written poetry and short fiction. Young is an Honorary Fellow at the University of Melbourne.

The Art of Reading

Damon Young

The Art of Reading

Damon Young

SCRIBE
Melbourne • London

Scribe Publications
18–20 Edward St, Brunswick, Victoria 3056, Australia
2 John St, Clerkenwell, London, WC1N 2ES, United Kingdom

Published in the UK by Scribe 2017
Published in North America by Scribe 2018
Originally published in Australia by Melbourne University Press 2016

Text design and typesetting by Megan Ellis
Printed and bound in the UK by CPI Group (UK) Ltd, Croydon CR0 4YY

Scribe Publications is committed to the sustainable use of natural resources and the use
of paper products made responsibly from those resources.

CiP records for this title are available from the British Library.

9781947534025 (US edition)
9781911344186 (UK edition)
9781925548099 (e-book)

scribepublications.com
scribepublications.co.uk
scribepublications.com.au

CONTENTS

For my parents, who began it all by reading to me.
And then by not reading to me.

A book is a thing among things, a volume lost among the volumes that populate the indifferent universe, until it meets its reader, the person destined for its symbols.

—Jorge Luis Borges, prologue to A Personal Library

One does not write for slaves.

—Jean-Paul Sartre, 'Why Write?'

LIBERATING PAGES

To my right is a small stained pine bookcase. It contains, among other things, my childhood.

Stacked in muted burgundy and khaki buckram are classics like *Aesop's Fables*, full of blunt aphorisms for 4-year-olds: 'To be well prepared for war is the best guarantee of peace'. Not far away is Richard Burton's translation of *The Book of the Thousand and One Nights*, with its formally phrased smut ('he laid his hand under her left armpit, whereupon his vitals and her vitals yearned for coition'). Still read after seven decades, my mother's octavo *The Magic Faraway Tree*—mystery, adventure and casual corporal punishment. I also have her *Winnie the Pooh*, printed the year she was born. Seventy years on, her grandson now has Eeyore days. ('Good morning, Pooh Bear ... If it is a good morning ... Which I doubt.') But most important for me, standing face out in black plastic leather and fake gold leaf, is *The Celebrated Cases of Sherlock Holmes*.

Holmes was my first literary world. Proudly bigger than anything read by my primary school peers, Conan Doyle's 800-page tome was a prop in my performance of superiority. This archaic lump of text helped me feel special. I was more clever, said the serious serif font, than the other 11-year-olds; more intellectually brave, said the ornamental binding, than my teachers.

Sherlock Holmes was a kind of existential dress-up—an adult I tried on for size. I made our common traits a uniform: social abruptness, emotional flight, pathological curiosity. In Conan Doyle's prose, this make-believe was more stylish than my clumsy boyhood persona. Take the first lines from *The Sign of the Four*: 'Sherlock Holmes took his bottle from the corner of the mantel-piece and his hypodermic syringe from its neat morocco case.' My detective was an addict: but with panache. (I kept a dictionary for words like 'morocco'. And 'panache'.)

Yet there was more to *The Celebrated Cases of Sherlock Holmes* than my pretence. What I finally took from Conan Doyle's mysteries was not savoir faire but freedom: the charisma of an independent mind. This Victorian London, with its shadows and blood, was *mine*. I winced as Holmes 'thrust the sharp point home, pressed down the tiny piston', but the needle and its rush were my own to invent. Watson's gentlemanly heroism, and Inspector Lestrade's mediocrity: all belonging to the little boy lying quietly on the flokati rug. So my Holmesian education was only partly about general knowledge—the symbolic pips of the Ku Klux Klan, the atmosphere of moors, the principles of deduction. It was also, more crucially, schooling in the exertion of my own psyche.

I willed this strange world into being, with help from Conan Doyle. The author was less like an entertaining uncle, and more like a conspirator. We met in private to secure my liberation from school's banality and home's atmosphere of violence.

Holmes was not my first book. I was already in that 'promised land', as Vladimir Nabokov put it in *Speak, Memory*, 'where ... words are meant to mean what they mean'. I learned to read with the 'Asterix' adventures, when my parents refused to voice the speech boxes. If I wanted the puns and fist-icuffs, I had to parse the text myself. Beside my bed there was also a lion who swallowed vegetable soup instead of rab-bits; dinosaurs against industrial pollution; and Ferdinand the pacifist bull. These were training and, later, distraction. Like Germaine Greer, who 'read for greed', I kept myself busy with words on paper—an urge closer to rapacity than curios-ity. These desires combined in 'Garfield', as I devoured car-toons and lasagne with equal urgency.

But with *The Celebrated Cases of Sherlock Holmes*, I had a new sense of greater mastery, and pleasure in this discovery. Part of me saw Holmes as a legendary historical hero, and I enjoyed what novelist Michael Chabon called the 'happy confusion' of fact and fiction. Another part of me, burgeoning and a little buzzed, was doing away with deference. I realised that these dark marks on paper were mine to ignore or inves-tigate, enrich or evade. It was with the junky detective that I first became aware of myself as something powerful: a reader.

SORCERY

Three decades later, my bookshelves are punctuated by discoveries of this imaginative independence. For these authors, the written word encouraged a new liberty: to think, perceive or feel with greater awareness.

Novelist William Gibson, whom I read as a teenager, is currently shelved in the garage between Ian Fleming's pubescent thrillers and Harry Harrison's galactic satire. Also roused by Sherlock Holmes as a boy, Gibson transformed his drab suburban neighbourhood into Victorian England, one brick wall at a time. 'I could imagine that there was an infinite number of similar buildings in every direction,' Gibson told *The Paris Review*, 'and I was in Sherlock Holmes's London.' Conan Doyle's stories were more than escapism or amusement for Gibson. They beckoned him to invent.

Two shelves under Gibson, Turkish novelist Orhan Pamuk recalled reading as relief from tears of boredom, and as a flight from confronting fact. In *Other Colours*, the novelist congratulated himself, as I did, on 'possessing greater depth than those who do not read'. This was partly juvenile boastfulness. But it was also an acknowledgement of the work involved: turning black text into an illuminated theatre. Pamuk wrote of the 'creator's bliss' he enjoyed as a child reader, putting his mind to work with words.

Two rooms behind and one century before Pamuk is American novelist Edith Wharton. Invited into her father's library as a child, she found a private sanctuary: a 'kingdom', as she put it. 'There was in me a secret retreat,' she wrote in *A Backward Glance*, 'where I wished no one to intrude.' This was more than withdrawal. With the poetry of Alfred Tennyson, Alexander Pope and Algernon Charles Swinburne, the criticism of John Ruskin, the novels of Walter Scott, Wharton played with exciting new themes and rhythms. She wrote about reading as a cultivation and celebration of her growing personality—what she called 'the complex music of my strange inner world'. The novelist believed that she became more fully herself in those yellowing pages.

Eighteenth century philosopher Jean-Jacques Rousseau, stacked two feet to the left of Wharton, read romantic novels late into the night with his widower father. The stories made him aware, for the first time, of his own mind. 'It is from my earliest reading,' he wrote in his *Confessions*, 'that I date the unbroken consciousness of my own existence.' The point is not only that Rousseau's emotions were encouraged by the novels, but also that he recognised them as *his*. And while the philosopher (characteristically) blamed fiction for his own histrionic bent, the melodrama arose chiefly out of little Jean-Jacques.

The shelf under Rousseau holds the modern philosopher, Jean-Paul Sartre. He discovered his literary authority in a sixth-floor apartment, looking down on Paris, his grandfather's books in his hands. Words gave the boy a certain mastery over himself: he was a demiurge, bestowing the world with life, in language. 'The Universe lay spread at my feet and each thing was humbly begging for a name,' he wrote, 'and giving it one was like both creating it and taking it.' Sartre also collected American westerns and detective comics, and their heroic caricature—lone brave man against the world—remained in his philosophy, decades later.

Simone de Beauvoir, close to Sartre in my library as in life, remembered the security of books. Not only because of their docile bourgeois morality, but also because they obeyed *her*. 'They said what they had to say, and didn't pretend to say anything else,' de Beauvoir wrote in *Memoirs of a Dutiful Daughter*, 'when I was not there, they were silent.' She recognised that they asked for conviction and artistry—from Simone, rather than simply from the authors. De Beauvoir called this 'the sorcery that transmutes printed symbols into stories': without a reader, the magic stops.

There is no one-size-fits-all discovery of literary power. Reading is thick with the quirks of era, family and psychology. Some, like Rousseau, find romantic urges. Others, like Sartre, find enlightenment domination. There can be pretence, narcissism and cowardice. (But enough about me.) In many cases, there is a longing for what philosopher Herbert Marcuse labelled 'holiday reality': an asylum from ordinariness. Charles Dickens wrote about this as his boyhood 'hope of something beyond that place and time'. But as Dickens' later popularity suggests, these moments of youthful bibliophilia also coincide with the discovery of clout. The child is becoming aware, not only of worlds populated with detectives, Gauls or bulls, but also of an 'I': the reader, whose consent and creativity brings these worlds into being. Reading is an introduction to a more ambitious mind.

TWO LIBERTIES

Jean-Paul Sartre, in *What is Literature?*, wrote: 'There is no art except for and by others'. The philosopher's argument was not that authors cannot enjoy writing for themselves; that every word is dashed off, hand aching, for tyrannical editors and audiences—what Henry James described in one letter as 'the devouring maw into which I … pour belated copy'. Instead, Sartre's point was that the text is only ever half finished by the writer. Without a reader, the text is a stream of sensations: dark and light shapes.

This does not mean ordinary life is a play of dumb necessity. Sensation always has *some* significance for humans—we are creatures of meaning, and the universe is never spied as a naked fact. But the world writ large does not refer to things fluently; the suggestions are often vague. 'The dim little meaning which dwells within it,' wrote Sartre of everyday sensation, 'a light joy, a timid sadness, remains imminent or trembles about it like a heat mist.' Ordinary life has a hazy atmosphere to it, whereas language illuminates brightly and sharply.

The letters achieve this by pointing beyond themselves—we read *through* the text, not off it. 'There is prose when the word passes across our gaze,' said Sartre, quoting the poet Paul Valéry, 'as the glass across the sun.' Words are portals of sorts: they frame reality, and become invisible as we peer.

Not all texts are as transparent as Sartre's ideal prose. Poetry can be more opaque. Take Seamus Heaney's 'The Bookcase'. It refers literally to the poet's library, but it also makes a spectacle of the English tongue. 'Ashwood or oakwood? Planed to silkiness / Mitred, much eyed-along, each vellum-pale / Board in the bookcase held and never sagged.' Alliteration, rhythm, metaphor: this is about a thing and its resonances, but it is also about language. Poetry puts on a show of words, just as painting displays colour, and music sound. Poetic phrases, wrote German philosopher Hans-Georg Gadamer, 'haul back and bring to a standstill the fleeting word that points beyond itself'.

Language can be translucent like amber or clear like Valéry's glass, but staring through it always asks for effort. Inscriptions or projections become words, which have meanings alongside their tone and cadence. This is what I first recognised in Sherlock Holmes: reading is always a transformation of sensation into sense. 'You have to make them all out of squiggles,' poet D Nurkse wrote, 'like the feelers of dead ants.'

For the reader, this means rendering a world: the intricate ensemble beyond the page. When Conan Doyle writes that the sun is visible 'through the dim veil which hangs over the great city', I recreate London. Not only the sky's spray of yellow and grey, but also the coal and commerce that make the metropolis 'great'. The newspaper reporting the death of Sherlock's client also evokes a community of middle-class readers from Cornwall to Northumberland, all participating in the imagined community of print. Waterloo Station, to which the victim was hurrying, suggests steam trains across England: taking passengers and parcels of *The Times* for men like Watson to read. All this I project behind the foreground prose. 'The objects represented by art,' as Sartre put it, 'appear against the background of the universe.' I piece together a cosmos from the author's fragments.

What this all reinforces is that writing cannot *make* anything happen. As an infant, earlier editions of *The Celebrated Cases of Sherlock Holmes* were wholly opaque to me: blocks of chewable stuff. And as an 11-year-old I was not forced to imagine Holmes in his 'velvet-lined arm-chair', pushing blow into his blood. I had to commit myself to the text; to consent to a kind of active passivity, in which I accepted Conan Doyle's words, then took responsibility for giving them some totality.

Reading requires some quantum of autonomy: no-one compels me to envisage their words. They are, at best, an invitation. Sartre phrases this as an 'appeal', and the idea makes sense of how little necessity is at play. Reading is always a meeting of two liberties: the artist's *and* the audience's.

AGAINST THE ODDS

In this light, it was false to say that my childhood is *in* the pine bookcase. It can seem this way, because old tomes prompt nostalgia. As Marcel Proust noted in *On Reading*, some memories of youth are lost in daily life, but regained in the pages we read during those years. 'They are the only calendars we have kept,' he writes, 'of days that have vanished'. But if I never read these volumes again, the recollections can become Proust's *temps perdu*: lost time. Whatever is most animated in the written word is only revived 'when the dead letter comes again into contact', as Hannah Arendt put it, 'with a life willing to resurrect it'.

This is a more general point. My books are just objects alongside other objects: pigment, glue, dead cellulose and cowskin. If they do not enter into specific relations with very specific objects—literate humans—then reading never happens. Reading in general might one day cease altogether. If the species known to itself as Homo sapiens becomes extinct, all these readable things—books, newspapers, tweets, billboards, roadside signs, subatomic initials on copper—will no longer be texts, strictly speaking. They will be lived in, eaten, buried, climbed upon, oxidised, but not read.

The ubiquity of script masks the rarity and fragility of reading. What you are doing right now is, cosmically speaking, against the odds.

GENIUSES AND SAINTS

An assumption: you enjoy this unlikely activity. For most readers, this is an untroubled devotion. It is easy to identify with playwright Tom Stoppard, who spent his bus fare on second-hand books, 'preferring the devil of hitchhiking to the deep blue sea of enduring half an hour bookless'. Identifying *why* we care is less straightforward.

Most obviously, reading is educational. This is why my parents intoned Blyton nightly, and why I spent so many afternoons sounding out *Miffy at the Gallery* to my daughter. An early introduction to the written word provides an enormous personal and political advantage. Researchers Anne Cunningham and Keith Stanovich reported that children's literature encourages a profuse vocabulary: 50 per cent more unusual words than the chatter of university students, or the most popular television. This lexical abundance then encourages *more* reading: positive feedback that begins well before school, and lasts a lifetime. Along the way, reading piles up vast stocks of otherwise obscure facts. Political gambits, scientific hypotheses, historical dramas: these become the taken-for-granted ground upon which citizens walk. Texts help to lay this foundation in childhood.

The written word can also boost psychological health and social connection. Studies suggest that a lifetime's reading, alongside company and exercise, can lessen dementia risk. Emory University researchers reported that participants reading a novel had more neural connectivity in the language and sensory motor regions of the brain. Lead author Gregory Berns wrote that 'reading a novel can transport you into the body of the protagonist'. What seems like an ethereal pursuit actually offers a visceral commingling. Research also suggests that literary fiction can contribute to a theory of mind, the idea we have of others' mental states. A New School for Social Research study revealed that reading authors like Don DeLillo or Anton Chekhov caused a brief but measurable jump in emotional intelligence: in this case, judging a stranger's mood from their eyes.

While it is flattering for bibliophiles to believe their pages guarantee a payoff, scepticism is warranted. Regular jogging might prevent mental decline far more reliably than reading Haruki Murakami on jogging. Some studies have small sample sizes or vague measures: brain scans say nothing about behaviour, or whether reading has unusual effects next to other pastimes. Others generalise too boldly about genres: does Chekhov have the same effects as Kazuo Ishiguro or Iris Murdoch? And even if DeLillo helps me guess someone's humour, I can be correct without being sympathetic or caring—bastards enjoy fiction too. (Some are authors.) Reading has demonstrable benefits, but it is not a machine for producing geniuses or saints.

This outlook also values reading as a means to an end. This is important, and covers many kinds of genuine worth: historical, philosophical, culinary, sexual. I pick up Conan Doyle to learn about Victorian London or Immanuel Kant to better comprehend modern ethical theory. Some read for symbolic capital, others for last-minute dinner recipes, others for orgasm ('a sort of ecstasy came over me after I had read for about an hour', said the heroine in eighteenth-century French bestseller *Thérèse the Philosopher*). There is no harm in highlighting the benefits of text, whether straightforward or subtle, scholarly or biological. But this approach can ignore how reading is an end in itself: an opportunity for experiences.

NO EXCUSES

Experience is vital: literally, to do with life. As philosopher John Dewey argued, my organic existence *is* experience: a to-and-fro between creature and milieu. I act upon things, and they upon me. I receive impressions, but my mind gives them colour, shape, significance. These prompt some reflex, habit or choice, which invites a response from the world. And so on. 'The career and destiny of a living being,' Dewey wrote, 'are bound up with its interchanges with its environment … in the most intimate way.' This whole interplay between myself and the cosmos is neither chaos nor perfect harmony, but unfolds in rhythms. We cannot know with absolute certainty what this universe is; cannot accept a naïve realism, which does away with philosophical doubt. But even here, the primacy of experience is clear: a creaturely play between self and other, which includes confusion about the edges of each.

Reading affords experiences. It does this, not by deputising me to solve crimes at Baker Street or doping me up to punch Roman centurions, but by tying signs to sense. Writing takes the stuff of daily life and crafts it into an innovative view of self and world. The 'dim little meaning' Sartre saw in ordinary sensation is given a new significance. Ideas are brought together in surprising ways; emotions moved from memory to fantasy; perceptions revivified or revised. While reading might not use every limb or organ, it draws on the fullness of life, rendering it with clarity, durability or vividness. 'Every work of art follows the plan of, and pattern of, a complete experience,' Dewey wrote, 'rendering it more intensely and concentratedly felt.'

This art need not be literary fiction or verse. While the best novels or poems are certainly transformative, disciplines like philosophy also offer experiences. The timbre of Aristotle's *Nicomachean Ethics* departs from that of Homer's *Iliad*, but Aristotle still offers a unique portrait of the cosmos, which includes its emotional atmospheres. Our doings and undergoings are not monopolised by any one literary form. From a quip on social media to biblical scrolls, writing gestures at some larger congress with the world; some universe beyond the glyphs. Whatever benefits reading offers, they are only gained *in* this experience: as part of a more general commingling with things.

With readers, this experience is often valued for its own sake. First, there is the pleasure of exertion. As David Hume noted in his *A Treatise of Human Nature*, mental effort is gratifying. We seek truth, he writes, because of 'the genius and capacity, which is employed in its invention and discovery'. This is as true of reading fiction as doing philosophy: either way, we are flexing psychological muscles.

But just as important is the world this labour offers. I read because I enjoy the experience of reading: the encounter with a refined and restored vision of life. This does not mean there is some invisible kernel of worth inside a book; that I can move quickly from my bliss to divinely given value, buried in dried cellulose and printer's ink. It means that I enjoy the experience *for* the experience, and nothing more. Perhaps it is the quickening of my speculative intellect as I read Alfred North Whitehead, or the curt beauty of a Deborah Levy phrase; perhaps it is the nostalgia prompted by Holmes, or the embarrassed recognition of myself in George Orwell's *Keep the Aspidistra Flying*; perhaps it is just the brief getaway, in a glib Star Trek novel, from the pain of living. This is why Virginia Woolf, in 'How Should One Read a Book?', portrayed God as a little jealous of literary souls. 'Look, these need no reward,' he proclaimed to Saint Peter in paradise. 'We have nothing to give them here. They have loved reading.' Reading is desirable for its own sake and, unless it causes harm, no excuses need be given.

THE DANCE

Reading is straightforwardly justified, but not so easily practised. Literary worth is only realised in the doing: it is active, not passive. Yes, reading involves some 'surrender', as Dewey puts it, to the text. Yet it also asks for mindful striving. It is not enough to simply be free—I have to exercise my liberty well. Reading artfully requires a fragile poise between proclivities: thought and feeling, spontaneity and habit, deference and critique, haste and slowness, boldness and caution, commitment and detachment.

Take Frank Miller's classic graphic novel *The Dark Knight Returns*, in which Batman takes apart a monstrous gang leader in combat. ('You don't … get it … boy. This isn't a mudhole … it's an operating table. And I'm the surgeon.') The stylised violence is a buzz, but the point of the fight is justice. So I am satisfied, rather than sulky, when it concludes with jail not murder. My passions are attuned to the tale and its mythos. Miller's story also invites analysis: of his libertarian politics, for example, or the ethics of training children in vigilantism. Yet to enjoy the novel, I cannot push the critique too far. I have to pretend nobody will recognise the tall, muscular billionaire in the mask, and that headbutting criminals one by one is a bona fide crime-prevention project. This care has to continue, regardless of my changing humours. If I miss political or ethical nuances in *The Dark Knight Returns* because I am tired or jittery, I cannot blame Miller. I have to claim my own fluctuations, without giving in to their conclusions. This tense equilibrium—between pleasure and revulsion, scrutiny and credulity, absorption and distance—also applies to other works in the genre. Ron Marz's *Green Lantern* #54, which uses a woman's gruesome murder as an easy heroic motive, rightly prompts disgust where Miller's macho pugilism does not. As a reader, my response is a negotiation, in which tendencies are continually checked and tweaked.

The word for this balance is 'virtue'. This word now has a lace curtain stuffiness to it; the mood of grim cautionary tales or a patriarch's finger wagging. Aristotle, who provided the original theory of virtues, does have moments of conservatism—philosopher Alasdair MacIntyre called him a 'supercilious prig'. But this is because of the Athenian scholar's aristocratic hauteur, not because his theories are wholly smug and contemptuous.

In classical Greek, the word for virtue was *aretē*: excellence. As Aristotle argued, an excellence is not a state of mind, since these change—it asks for a life's striving, not a single moment. It is not simply conceptual, though it is rational. Virtue is not just an emotion, though it does involve feelings. And it is not just a reflex, though it is a custom of sorts. Each excellence is what Aristotle called a *hexis*: a tendency, disposition or inclination. It suggests readiness or preparedness. I am virtuous when I routinely respond well in changing circumstances, and do so knowingly and willingly. So literary *aretē* is not innate, but nor is it artificial. Like reading itself, a good *hexis* is a potential we are born with, but have to realise with regular toil.

For Aristotle, every virtue is a mean between two extremes: a deficiency and an excess. It is cowardly to give up on Fyodor Dostoyevsky's *Crime and Punishment* because it is discomfiting; foolhardy to keep reading if it will push me to rabidly bludgeon my landlady. Courage is the mean: I recognise the threat to my bourgeois equilibrium, but press on because the novel promises a psychologically rich experience. Aristotle's three-part scheme is not always convincing, and some virtues—like temperance and justice—fail to fit the blueprint neatly. But in general, this pagan idea of excellence makes sense of the balance the written word requires. This is why Virginia Woolf called reading, in her notes on James Joyce, 'almost a school for character': it provides a chance for virtues to thrive.

There is no law here, as virtue shifts with text and context. This is one of the strengths of Aristotle's outlook: he refuses to give a rule. 'The man of education,' he wrote, 'will seek exactness so far in each subject as the nature of the thing admits.' *Aretē* can only be developed with experience—it is a knack, a know-how, not an axiom. To read well, I have to *read*: widely and carefully, mindful of my powers and responsibilities.

This does not mean observing myself, as if I were divided into two selves, one looking at phrases, another inspecting this looking. As philosopher Gilbert Ryle noted, the 'I' is always tardy with its scrutiny. We treat our own behaviour as we do someone else's: something to be examined, criticised, praised or ignored. But there is only one consciousness, and it cannot concentrate on itself—what it heeds are memories, 'logically condemned to eternal penultimacy'. The virtues of reading ask not for schizoid surveillance, but for honest recollection and reflection.

Yet I can never be perfectly emancipated from bias. One of Aristotle's points is that I *am* bias: a tangle of tendencies, which compete and collude. I can reflect on these, but I cannot ever be free from the 'irrational' part of the soul, as Aristotle put it. Reflection is itself a kind of leaning; a bent, which is strengthened or weakened with effort. By reading freely today I develop tomorrow's prejudices—the point is to develop them conscientiously. Friedrich Nietzsche once referred to the best scholarship and prose as a dance of 'suppleness and strength', but reading also asks for this: a gruelling but light-footed agility.

A CULT OF COLOPHONS

Despite civilisation's glut of signs, the virtues of reading are rarely celebrated. Reading well is treated as a rudimentary skill, not a lifelong ambition; not a creative talent to tenaciously enrich and enhance.

This contrasts with the popular writing industry: degrees, short courses, workshops, masterclasses, centres, festival panels. Newspapers and magazines run 'how-to' pages: George Orwell on clear prose, George RR Martin on fantasy, Philip Pullman on lists ('My main rule is to say no to things like this, which tempt me away from my proper work.'). There is even Jane Austen on literary success. (Confession: I wrote it.) Many promise not only technical know-how, but also tricks for convincing editors to publish and audiences to buy.

In this, the art of reading often takes second place to the fantasy of publication. One survey reported that, in the United States, eight out of ten people wanted to write a book—a startling figure, even if only half right. Yet for all their hankering after authorial identity, many are not bibliophiles. The Pew Research Center found that a quarter of Americans had not read a book in the previous year. As writer and translator Tim Parks noted, authorship has become a glamorous professional persona, rather than a craft. 'It's rather as if the spontaneous Romanticism of the nineteenth-century poets,' he wrote, 'had become a job description.' However at odds this might be with the daily discipline of professional writers, the caricature abides. Novelist Flannery O'Connor's curmudgeonly observation seems right: 'They are interested in being a writer, not in writing. They are interested in seeing their names at the top of something printed, it matters not what.' A cult of colophons.

Perhaps this is a mark of all literate and leisured communities. Imperial Rome had a small but animated culture of letters. In the first century, the poet Martial complained of harassment by an aspiring author. 'You read to me as I stand, you read to me as I sit,' he spat, 'you read to me as I run, you read to me as I shit.' The impression is of endless, often egotistic scrawling and orating. Martial himself wrote over a thousand epigrams, often riffing on the work of his predecessors. Martial's younger contemporary Juvenal satirised the sickness of *cacoethes scribendi*: the malignant urge to write. Roman patrons offered praise, he complained, but no cash—glory did not pay for wine. 'Yet still we keep at it, ploughing a dusty furrow,' Juvenal wrote, 'turning the seashore up with our sterile coulter.' In a poem nodding back to Juvenal, American doctor and poet Oliver Wendell Holmes Sr made a similar diagnosis some eighteen centuries later. Even if all the world were stationery, he wrote in 'Cacoethes Scribendi', every ocean filled with ink then drained, 'Still would the scribblers clustered round its brink / Call for more pens, more paper, and more ink'.

Whether *cacoethes scribendi* is ancient or modern, the problem is not writing itself. It is absurd to applaud reading while turning our backs on authors. And amateur composition can also be valuable. As philosopher RG Collingwood argued, writing can be therapeutic. Expression, whether in poetry or philosophy, offers a chance for psychological lucidity. This is neither automatic nor always entertaining, but it can overcome what Collingwood calls 'corruption of consciousness': the refusal of reality. This remedy need not be public, as letters and diaries are textual laboratories too. Learning to write can also cultivate respect for others' talent and achievements—with proficiency comes some connoisseurship. German philosopher-poets Johann Wolfgang von Goethe and Friedrich Schiller pointed out that connoisseurs respect the effort of art, while dilettantes are restless hoarders; mere collectors of others' invisible effort. So those trivialised as dabblers are as critical in literature as they are in sport or painting. By learning to write, I can become more familiar with myself (or at least my illusions), and more generous with others' labour.

The problem is that this zeal seldom applies to reading. It is rarely acknowledged that I might be deft with de Beauvoir's 'sorcery', yet fail to deploy this magic *well*; that I might be a gifted writer, but use my reader's freedom clumsily or viciously.

AMNESIA AND DIZZINESS

The neglect of reading is, in some ways, straightforward. Most obviously, literacy is usually a childhood accomplishment, which becomes automatic. We are born recognising almost nothing in the world, but slowly we associate certain colours, shapes and movements with things. A rounded rectangle of black and gold becomes 'book', along with countless oblongs of cream white and glaucous blue. Each impression is actually new, but we learn to see regularities in the flux. The same is true of reading: this knack for joining perceptions with things is coopted. Lines first become names ('ay', 'bee', 'see'), then sounds, which combine to call up ideas and emotions. 'We are literate not by virtue of a divine intervention,' wrote Oliver Sacks in *The Mind's Eye*, 'but through a cultural invention and a cultural selection that makes a brilliant … new use of a preexisting neural proclivity.' Because this happens immediately and easily for literate adults, it is easy to forget its novelty and wonder. The first exuberance is lost, along with the willingness to develop this new sense further.

The art of reading is also largely invisible to others. 'I realized that no one … could enter my reading-space,' wrote Alberto Manguel in *A History of Reading*, 'and that nothing except my own will could enable anyone else to know.' Even if I read aloud—as was the custom in the classical and medieval eras—and with an audience, this display can be deceptive. Much of what makes reading so psychologically rich is private, and might be at odds with my public persona. A charismatic performer can give a semblance of masterful reading—witness Henry Crawford in Jane Austen's *Mansfield Park*—but there is a chasm between acting and parsing. I can chat about a novel, and display my take: attentive or restless, informed or ignorant, approving or scornful. But much of reading withdraws from inspection.

This makes reading less suitable for swaggering or preening displays. Yes, I can use text as a status symbol, as sociologist Pierre Bourdieu suggests. My gold-rimmed copy of *The Celebrated Cases of Sherlock Holmes* was my own bad investment in a cultural market. Still, this kind of play for power says nothing about *how* I interpret the words. For this reason, reading is a quieter talent. For those who seek cultural capital, writing is a cannier down payment.

But there is more to forgetting the art of reading than its early origins, or unseen inwardness. Reading can also prompt uneasiness. Not simply because of monsters like *Beowulf*'s Grendel or *Lolita*'s Humbert Humbert, but because liberty is discomfiting: my life is mine to justify, and no-one can do it on my behalf. I cannot escape what Bourdieu called 'social space', and I am a specific animal, with specific physiological needs. But what do I make of these, and of myself? There is no grand cosmic hieroglyph, pointing the way from life to death. There is no final answer to the question of humanity. This, argued philosopher Martin Heidegger in *Being and Time*, causes *Angst*, or anxiety.

Angst is not just fear; not flinching at this or that threat. Angst is a mood, which spreads over the world. Suddenly existence seems false, illusory or simply pointless. I rarely feel this foreboding, because I am busy with logistics. But occasionally I am reminded that there are no perfect personal certainties; that my ideals and values are mine to claim or criticise, celebrate or mock. 'Everyday familiarity,' as Heidegger put it, 'collapses.' In this mood, I cannot rest on gods or nature: the weight of life is mine to bear. Along with this burden comes vertigo—the dizzy awareness of what is beneath me: almost nothing. Anxiety is an uncanny combination of heaviness and lightness, horror and exhilaration.

Words evoke this angst because they reveal my role in rendering worlds; they show up all the possibilities I ignore in favour of safe actuality. If the reader is as free as the author, then there is no escape from this play of potential. The page is only a brief certainty between human ambiguities. Giddiness arises as I become aware of my responsibility for affirming one world and not another, and the fragility of whatever is chosen. Every string of letters can be an existential challenge.

This dizziness is another reason for the cult of the author: it allows us to stop the play of signs. As philosopher Michel Foucault noted, the writer can be a way of making reading safe. Not the actual writer, with her royalty cheques and lumbar soreness, but the idea of the writer—what Foucault called the 'author function'. The author function is not a person, but a way of managing meaning, which arises out of social and psychological forces. It is simpler to believe that 'Marcel' in *Remembrance of Things Past* is actually Marcel Proust, or that the 'I' in Nikos Kazantzakis's mythological memoir *Report to Greco* is the moustachioed loather of bonsai. The author becomes a way of simplifying the text. The words come from this Frenchman or Greek, and they simply reflect his homosexuality or impotence, nothing more.

Foucault's point is not that the author's life and motives are always irrelevant. Anything intertwined with the knot of creation is germane: plague in Plato's *Republic*, Judaism and migration in Superman, syphilis in Nietzsche's *Ecce Homo*. The author can certainly become 'figured in the carpet' of the text, as Roland Barthes put it. Foucault's point is that the author is only one way of reading among many, which highlights some meanings, and hides others, often while staying hidden itself. He called this a 'principle of thrift in the proliferation of meaning'. By fixating on authorship, I can give myself the gift of obviousness, with all the complacency this affords: the work just means *this*, end of story.

So the reader's freedom is not simply forgotten. It is shrugged off because of the prickly doubt that words can cause. Whether in scripture, newspaper columns or graphic novels, easy certainty is sought in the pages. Words become someone else's job: the author is celebrated as a lone genius or blamed for their Grub Street hackery. The reader's potencies are denied, along with a chance to exercise them more artfully.

CONVIVIALITY

The Art of Reading is a reply to this repression—a reminder of the reader's power to realise worlds. Each chapter highlights a specific virtue: curiosity, patience, courage, pride, temperance and justice. This leaves out many of the classical excellences, and for good reason. Aristotle's magnificence is better for moneyed nobles than bibliophiles, while liberality makes little literary sense. The Greek philosopher's truthfulness is covered by pride, while even temper is celebrated throughout. Augustine urged good Christians to pick up the Bible for love, but treated most writing with contempt. For him, it was better to avoid the written word altogether, than to fail at adoring God ('a curse is pronounced on him who places his hope in man'). Likewise, faith and hope are too bound to religious cosmology and morality to help secular readers. Of the cardinal virtues, humility is part of healthy pride, while chastity in letters resembles temperance. (Though I recommend polyamory with books.) Like the pagan and Christian catalogues, this list is partial and idiosyncratic but not arbitrary. It reflects what I esteem.

The Art of Reading reflects on the nature of writing, but it is a long way from Jacques Derrida's *Of Grammatology*, which doggedly sniffs out and digs up Western metaphysics. My interest is not the history of being, but character—however vague and volatile this 'I' might be. I argue that some inter-pretations are better than others, but this is no interpretive manual, in the style of Augustine's *On Christian Teaching*. I have forsaken encyclopaedic mastery for biographical hon-esty: my consciousness is partly what I have read and how I have read it. While I have read adventurously—from specula-tive realism to superhero noir, Heidegger to Heinlein—I have my own prejudices: authors, genres and styles. Sometimes I have overcome these biases, and disclosed my dubious self. Sometimes I have justified my bent. The point is not to defend a final exegesis, but to provide a public reflection on this often private art.

This confession is important because virtues, as Alasdair MacIntyre noted, are best developed communally. If reading is a confrontation between two liberties, then reading *well* asks for a third: other readers, from whom I receive rival or exotic impressions of life.

This is partly why literary criticism is so fundamental. Critics are caricatured as snooty gatekeepers, anaesthetised pedants, or parasites—and some live up to the stereotypes. But the best critics exemplify the art of reading. They do not simply shed light on works. They also reveal the prejudices— clarifying or obfuscating, charitable or mean, curious or numbed to novelty—we bring to works, and the visions of life these promote. American essayist HL Mencken argued that the critic is a 'catalyser': instead of two chemical substances, the critic works between a text and its reader. 'It is his business to provoke the reaction,' Mencken wrote, 'between the work of art and the spectator.' Sometimes, this is true: the critic helps an untutored or uncertain audience. Works that are bafflingly foreign in era, language or sensibility become more familiar. But critics can also prompt reactions in readers who are erudite and assured, *because* they are erudite and assured— they need their conceits relaxed. The finest critical studies can make a philosophical contribution, loosening a white-knuckle grip on taken-for-grantedness.

Professionals have no monopoly on this role. Yes, the better critics make it their business to walk a tightrope between sobriety and play, I and thou, text and context—all while trying to enjoy the view. But they do so because of a more basic drive to respond sensitively and intelligently to words. This is why critics choose the vocation (or are chosen by it)—they savour the art of reading as much as writing. Their willingness to make 'eloquent obeisance' to greater talents, as critic Geordie Williamson put it, arises partly from their own revelled-in proficiencies. And these gratifying talents are not confined to magazine cubicles or academic seminars. The strife of interpretations occurs in metropolitan literary festivals and suburban book clubs; at the café bench or domestic dinner table. Not everyone is a critic, but every reader can employ criticism in company—not simply to catch out authors, but to keep an eye on themselves.

The Art of Reading is an exercise in this gregarious reading: a reminder of freedom and the rewards of its adventurous deployment. It is also my personal appeal to this very same liberty.

CURIOSITY

The Infinite Library

This chapter existed before I was born.

There are twenty-six letters in English, and a handful of punctuation marks. In any work of this length, there are only so many ways to shuffle the glyphs. Uncountable, perhaps—but limited. Most will be gobbledegook, but many will be legible and plausible. Some will include this very paragraph, only the word 'chapter' will read 'sardine'; in others, every character will be a 'z', except for the word 'gobbledegook'; in others, every thirteenth word will be 'Sinestro'. Regardless of how innovative I am with ideas or prose, nothing profoundly new can be invented. I am only ever choosing one combination of symbols from a seemingly endless catalogue.

In the great restaurant of literature, all writing is à la carte.

So suggested the Argentine author Jorge Luis Borges, in his short story 'The Library of Babel'. Borges described an infinite library, made up of identical rooms: hexagonal, with bookcases along four walls. Stacked in the shelves of each are over six hundred books. The rooms go on forever. Generations are born and die within this bibliotecha, and Borges described them wandering from cell to cell, many in search of *the* book: a 'total book', which provides a guide to the whole world. Some citizens are overjoyed: there must be books of perfect science and prophecy, describing the universe with wonder, and their lives with candour. Some are melancholy or mad: what chance is there of finding anything but banality or nonsense among the countless pages? The narrator is tired and has little hope. 'I believe I have mentioned the suicides,' he wrote, 'more and more frequent over the years.' He suspects humanity will be extinct soon, and only the library will continue, 'illuminated, solitary, infinite, perfectly motionless'.

Borges's is an eerie vision of infinity, which mocks the calm of library catalogues—from Dewey Decimal to delirium. It also thumbs its nose at authorial supremacy, as every masterpiece is just a copy from the master plan. In fact, Borges's fable itself is a new version of an old idea. As he noted in 'The Total Library', the basic concept has been around for at least two millennia. Aristotle gestured at it, Cicero formulated its premise, and others—from Blaise Pascal, to Thomas Huxley, to Lewis Carroll—developed the arguments for or against. So Babel simply repeats, in austere prose, an ancient notion of repetition. The same image recurred in Borges's childhood and fiction: fear of multiplication. 'Mirrors and copulation are abominable,' he wrote in 'Tlön, Uqbar, Orbis Tertius', 'because they increase the number of men.' The overall picture is what Borges called 'a subaltern horror': a universe of timeless absurdity, containing only enough beauty to discomfit with its rarity. And at its centre: words.

PARADISE

Yet for all this dread, Borges was a bibliophile extraordinaire. 'I had always imagined Paradise,' he wrote in 'Blindness', 'as a kind of library.' His father's books initiated his literary identity. 'Father's library,' wrote biographer Edwin Williamson, 'became his playground. ' Two of Borges's few formal jobs were in libraries: as a young man in a local institution (he catalogued too fast, annoying the other workers) and in his fifties as director of the National Library in Buenos Aires. While the author was blind and often housebound, he still visited second-hand bookstores regularly. Argentine-born Alberto Manguel, who worked in one of those shops as a boy, remembered Borges's visit. 'He was almost completely blind and yet he refused to carry a cane,' Manguel wrote, 'and he would pass a hand over the shelves as if his fingers could see the titles.' In the National Library, Borges had two revolving bookcases, filled with specific books in unchanging order: from a well-thumbed but refurbished *Webster's Encyclopedic Dictionary of the English Language*, to volumes of Norse poetry. Almost sixty, the blind director began to teach himself Anglo-Saxon, with the help of students. 'I have lost the visible world,' he wrote, 'but now I am going to recover another, the world of my distant ancestors, these tribes of men who rowed across the stormy northern seas.' Books were an adventure.

It is important not to conflate narrator, author and man. Borges himself noted the uncanny divide between human being and literary persona. In 'Borges and I', he confessed that the latter was 'the one things happen to', and the man was like a biological battery: keeping the author powered. The man was important, but what lived on was the work; and, beyond the work, the language; and beyond language, some mysterious eternity. He toyed with this idea elsewhere, pointing out that Dante did not fully understand the poetry he was given to write. 'The machinery of the world,' he wrote in 'Inferno, I, 32', 'is much too complex for the simplicity of men.' In the same way, he wrote of the 'emptiness' of Shakespeare and God: both creators. The point, running through so many of Borges's works, is that individuals are less important, and more mercurial, than they seem. Literature is not neat autobiography, and there is no simple 'Jorge Luis Borges' on the page.

Still, Borges's essays and tales portray a mania for read-ing—in this, the persona does not lie. As a man, Borges savoured conversation and was known later as an entertain-ing raconteur on American tours. The topic of so many tête-à-têtes with friends and students was not gossip, but what he did alone in his study or bedroom: reading. 'I have always come to things,' he wrote in *The New Yorker*, 'after coming to books.' He compared studying to falling in love.

His written works suggest this adoration. Not in their classical style—which is notably austere—but in their playful jumping from work to work, author to author. In 'On the Cult of Books', Borges demonstrates the slow metamorphosis of text into a sacred artefact. Whereas the ancients like Plato were often suspicious of the written word, French poet Stéphane Mallarmé wrote that 'everything in the world exists to end up in a book'. Others, like Roger Bacon, declared that nature itself *was* a book of sorts, with creatures as its alphabet. Along the way, Borges moves from Homer, to Cervantes, to Bernard Shaw, Augustine of Hippo, the Koran, Kabbalistic treatises, Thomas Carlyle and more. The essay is not only an argument for the sanctity of literature, but also a demonstration of this very worship: the library that is Borges's awesome universe. In another essay, 'Coleridge's Dream', he described artworks with oneiric origins, chiefly Coleridge's poem on Kubla Khan's palace. Borges pointed out that the citadel itself was reportedly conceived in a dream. He ends with a suggestion that each reverie brings us closer to 'an archetype not yet revealed to mankind': some ideal blueprint, with which humanity builds its fantasies. In making his argument, Borges nodded to poets John Keats and Swinburne, anthropologist Havelock Ellis, historian Bede and the philosopher Alfred North Whitehead—all in four pages, in my edition. Borges's use of literary sources suggests a continuity of ideas and phrases, connecting alien places and times. In skipping so cheerily between them, he reveals the enduring principles behind lonely facts.

SKIPPING WITH PLATO AND BUDDHA

This is partly a philosophical commitment. Borges gave more credence to mind than physicality; more to speculation than to fact. His willingness to hop from age to age, country to country, came from an awareness of greater possibilities. For someone with an eye on the teeming cosmos, things can always be otherwise. One glyph can change a sentence; one reader, a proof. Only the Library of Babel continues. It makes sense to restlessly move between artworks, never believing that any one is perfect.

Alongside this Platonic bent was Borges's nihilism: a belief in the ultimate nullity of things. This is why he was suspicious of the ego, and saw himself, like Dante and Shakespeare, as empty. Literary scholar Jason Wilson, in his critical biography of Borges, aphorised the author's outlook neatly: 'We are all hungry ghosts, without essential identity'.

Borges was not a fully-fledged Buddhist, but his writings echoed the Asian philosophy's scepticism about definite, durable things—including the 'I'.

These two traditions, idealism and Buddhism, came together in Borges's favourite philosopher: Arthur Schopenhauer, whose essays addressed 'the riddle of the universe'. Because of this vision of the world, Borges's love of the written word was marked by a refusal of straightforward reality, and a genuine humility about his own importance. He never took texts, or what they prompted, for granted.

The overall impression from Borges's works is delight: the thrill of insights gained through reading. A particular *kind* of insight, no doubt: metaphysical and psychological, rather than political or scientific. But within the walls of Borges's epic bibliotheca were multitudes. (He was a Whitman fan.) He wrote of his joy in intellectual discovery and lauded 'the pleasure of thinking'. He defended the value of crime fiction— not for its titillating gore, but for its cerebral striving. He believed that these kinds of detective tales, from Poe to Conan Doyle, were committed to a fantasy: that abstract reasoning mattered. 'It is safeguarding order,' he wrote in 'The Detective Story', 'in an era of disorder.' Generally in Borges's work, the mind revels in its own inventions. Not because it ought to, but because it can. This is a fondness, not for practical nous or experimental precision, but for puzzles, games, whimsies and jokes. He enjoyed exercising his intellect, leaping from one textual stepping stone to another, smiling as the river kept expanding. Borges was, in a word, curious.

EXERTING GENIUS

Scottish philosopher David Hume, whom Borges read carefully, devoted a chapter to curiosity in his *Treatise of Human Nature*. Hume referred to curiosity as 'the love of truth', though this description can be misleading. It is not desire for facts or even for verity, but for the labour of discovering them. What is 'most pleasant and agreeable', Hume wrote, is when we 'fix our attention or exert our genius'. Obviously not just any truth will do: easy puzzles are dull. Borges, for example, might have simply counted the references to dreams in Coleridge's poems, then given them a score. This might have been perfectly correct, but boring. What prompted and rewarded Borges's curiosity was the suggestion of an ideal thread, tied between a Mongolian general and a Lake poet, or between God, De Quincey and Swift. For Hume, this achievement was savoured for its own sake, not for career or cash.

This does not mean curiosity is a 'pure' interest, above the clay of society and psyche. By involving pleasure, Hume reveals that intellectual curiosity requires some bent: the partialities that nudge us to peer more closely, or look past the obvious. So-called 'disinterested' research is still a leaning of sorts. The point is that Hume's curiosity is neither utilitarian nor necessarily about duty.

This contrasts with literary pride. A scholar can be proud of her careful analysis of mirrors in Borges's stories, for example, without enjoying the labour itself. It might simply be a professional obligation, diligently completed—the literature review before the year's requisite publications count. Whereas curiosity in Hume's sense is about the pursuit of truth as an end in itself, not the 'I' that does the pursuing. It is a thrill in the doing, *for* the doing.

Hume also argued that curiosity asks for some importance, because this aids focus. 'When we are careless and inattentive,' said Hume, 'the same action of the understanding has no effect upon us'. This sense of worth changes with character. So Borges's literary values departed from his macho library coworkers'. (One thought it a funny coincidence that a catalogued author was *also* named Jorge Luis Borges.) But Hume's point is clear: curiosity is encouraged by the greatness of the truth involved. Big things—infinities, dream worlds, centuries-old secrets—kept Borges with his nose in tomes. It does not matter, said Hume, whether or not these actually are a big deal. Their metaphysical grandeur or political usefulness might be wholly made-up. The chief thing is their psychological gravity: weight, which keeps the mind pulled in.

Borges read constantly and passionately, but he cared little about scuttlebutt. In fact, his late, doomed marriage to Elsa Astete Millán was made all the more awkward by his new wife's interest in gossip. (It was suggested by a friend that Borges wed Elsa because he knew her decades earlier: like the plot of a novel.) In the *Treatise*, Hume made a helpful distinction between curiosity proper and what he described as an 'insatiable desire of knowing the actions and circumstances of … neighbours'. Gossips are often caricatured as novelty chasers, but Hume argued that their longing actually comes from a fear of the new. Their little world is neat and still, and they find change troublesome. 'Too sudden and violent a change is unpleasant to us, and,' he wrote, 'however any objects may in themselves be indifferent, yet their alteration gives uneasiness.' Craving rumours or scandals is, in this light, a way to stave off discomfiting uncertainty.

When Borges picked up Dante's *Purgatorio* or HG Wells's *The Invisible Man*, he was not after gossip: the consolation of reliable facts. His Buddhist-like insistence on transience and idealist wariness of matter, left him antsy. Borges looked for predictability on his office shelves, but not in the contents of his library. Hence his insistence on coming back to works, after years: a way to reveal new relationships between and within the covers. 'I prefer rereading to reading,' Borges told an audience at the University of Maine, 'since when you reread, you are delving down.'

ADVENTURES IN BABEL

It is important not to gild Borges's literary lily. He had, as John Updike put it in 'The Author as Librarian', a 'fervent narrowness'. He was dismissive of many brilliant works, particularly those by women. His precious canon of English literature lacked Jane Austen, George Eliot, Virginia Woolf, Iris Murdoch. When asked which female authors he celebrated, he answered: 'I think I would limit myself to one, to Emily Dickinson'. He showed little interest in social and political scholarship, which might have made his clumsy grip on Argentina a little more deft. When Borges was charged with ignoring his murdered compatriots under the juntas, his reported reply was damning: 'I don't read newspapers'. Biographer James Woodall also described him as 'a wretched historian'. Overall, Borges's pleasure as a reader was idiosyncratic and sometimes idiotic, in the ancient Greek sense: privative and egocentric.

Nonetheless, Borges's curiosity was, within these limits, exemplary. Hence his charm for first-time readers, which Clive James called 'an intellectual adventure guaranteed to thrill the young'. What the Argentine, with his Babel and infinities, adds to Hume's theory is the importance of otherwise; of the 'maybe' that waits beyond every certain phrase. To be genuinely curious is to be a little jittery; to see the current page as one of many possibilities, interpreted in light of many other possibilities. This is neither haste nor arrogance—as with Borges, it can work hand in hand with patience and dignity. A little humility is vital: because the possibilities are practically endless, there is no final reading. Curiosity allows the reader to be gratified by this discovery, and revel in the quest. 'The true hero of the Library of Babel,' wrote Umberto Eco, 'is not the library itself, but its Reader ... on the move, adventurous, restlessly inventive.'

THE CHARM OF THE ACTUAL

Perhaps most vital in curiosity is resistance to the torpor of being: the way what already and notably exists seems *necessary*. The curious reader treats the text as contingent, simply one choice among many. This is not the hack critic's gambit—a gotcha move that censures an author for writing 'the wrong' novel or poem. Instead, curiosity is an appreciative sensitivity to the pliability of creation; the sense that every artefact is a fraction.

Batman, for example, has canonical heft: one of the totemic heroes of the era, whose stories have been adapted, lampooned and simply copied for decades. Within the super-hero genre, various popular protagonists—Green Arrow, Moon Knight, Iron Man—are often trivialised as Batman knock-offs. This is to say nothing of the Dark Knight dop-pelgängers within the official universe: franchisees from China, Russia, France and Australia. If we go back a century, we find heroes like Zorro, the Shadow and Jean-Paul Sartre's beloved Nick Carter (*Le Grand Détective Américain*). And behind these, the broader genre of detective fiction, including Sherlock Holmes and the works of Borges's favourites Wilkie Collins and Edgar Allen Poe. For all his popularity, Batman is only one page in the book of masked, nocturnal vigilantes or detectives with preternatural logic and expensive gadgets.

Once this is recognised, Batman is no longer the original; the plate from which all others are minted. Instead, the hero represents one answer to readers' needs; or, more correctly, many answers, as he is written in many ways. Batman is less a single character, and more the name for a family of traits—they share not some essential soul but what Ludwig Wittgenstein, in his *Philosophical Investigations*, called 'family resemblances'. Most incarnations of the Dark Knight lost their parents when young; but Batman Thomas Wayne lost his son. Most do not kill, but the 'goddamn Batman' burns thugs to death then has sex beside their smoking corpses. Most are taciturn and brutal; but the 1960s television Batman is more chatty and playful. Almost all wear black, blue and grey; but 'Rainbow Batman' is a sartorial riot. Each story is its own version of an adaptation that is composed of nothing more than adaptations: authenticity is born of verisimilitude, not a primordial essence.

Curiosity need not be about tracing influence or iteration in this way. It might be fact-finding: the actual career-span of a vigilante, for example. (A few years before crippling injuries, according to neuroscientist E Paul Zehr.) It might be biographical: the legal and ethical conflict behind the Batman brand. Obviously, it need not be about superheroes at all—these iconic characters simply reveal the play of invention more clearly. By definition, curiosity often has unpredictable results. Whether we are reading Alan Moore on Batman or John Stuart Mill on liberty, Edith Wharton on haut-bourgeois

New York or Ursula K Le Guin on dragons, the point is to keep pressing on the edges of the literary world.

Curiosity might seem to diminish literary pleasure, because it dashes the spell of uniqueness or perfection. It reveals antecedents, parallels, agendas and simple errors. Certainly, I cannot read HP Lovecraft with the same thrill now, having traced the marks of vulgar xenophobia in his fiction. My innocent enjoyment of Borges himself was marred by the revelations of his reactionary politics and casual racism. His otherworldliness seems as sinister as it is high-minded. The artistry of many novels can seem false when their real-life equivalents are demonstrated: passages from Virginia Woolf's *Mrs Dalloway* or Simone de Beauvoir's *The Mandarins* lifted from diaries. But chasing these facts was itself fun. As Hume noted, scholarship is something like a hunt, in which we start to care about victory even if we are aloof from the sport. 'In the heat of the action we acquire such an attention to this end,' he wrote, 'that we are very uneasy under any disappointments, and are sorry when we ... miss our game. ' I did not *want* to find fault with Lovecraft or Borges, but I was wholly content as I chased my prey.

Far from undermining specialness, curiosity can sometimes intensify the aura of innovation. By showing the possibilities that surround any one text, they highlight the specificity of the craft: of all the stories or arguments, characters and atmospheres, plots and phrases, the author deployed *these*. The move from formal catechism to sensual soliloquy in James Joyce's *Ulysses*; the 'hot' in Ted Hughes's 'The Thought-Fox', with its suggestion of musky vitality: 'sudden sharp hot stink of fox'. Each work achieves its power with these choices. Joyce's chapter is not simply a weary riff on Catholic schoolroom primers. Hughes's animal says nothing, unlike the burnt fox in the dream that prompted the poem ('it said: "Stop this—you are destroying us."') Each work might have been written otherwise, and the curious reader discovers this: fossicking about in the rooms of Borges's infinite library. It takes a sense of brooding possibility to recognise the charm of the actual.

REVEREND AND AWESOME

It is easy to laud curiosity—one of the few universally hailed modern virtues. But like all dispositions, it can err. Because it leapfrogs the immediate, curiosity can leave the actual too far behind. We read inventively, but end up squinting from a distance—the work itself becomes blurred. Intellectual exertion becomes a pleasurable flight from the details of the text and its author's choices. Curiosity can also become a way of avoiding *why* we are curious; a way of ignoring our own quirks and flaws.

Take Martin Heidegger, one of the twentieth century's most prominent philosophers. Heidegger's chief interest was ontology: the study of being, of what 'is' is. He was also a petty anti-Semite and Nazi sympathiser, facts that have equally obscured and illuminated his challenging works. At his best, he offers profound surprise: a reminder that there is something rather than nothing, and that this is marvellous. While rightly critical of Heidegger's political and ethical failings, philosopher and critic George Steiner described him as 'the great master of astonishment', who 'put a radiant obstacle in the path of the obvious'.

Heidegger was partly responsible for a renaissance of the Presocratics: philosophers who worked in the sixth and fifth centuries before Christ. Heidegger took the surviving

fragments of these ancient philosophers' oeuvres and interpreted them in bold new ways—what he called 'the authentic
truth of the primordially Greek words'.

One of Heidegger's memorable studies was of Parmenides
of Elea. Arguably the most important Presocratic thinker,
Parmenides was in his prime during the early fifth century.
His reflections on the unity, ubiquity and eternity of being
influenced Plato, whose intellectual legacy bankrolled much
of Western philosophy and theology. In Plato's *Theaetetus*,
Socrates describes Parmenides as 'reverend and awesome,'
and remembers his profound nobility. A generation later,
Aristotle singled out Parmenides for his 'insight', devoting
parts of *Physics* to overturning his basic ideas about
existence. Aristotle also believed that Parmenides drove
the development of Greek atomism, as philosophers tried
to overcome his powerful arguments—a development that
encouraged Enlightenment scientists two millennia later.
Parmenides made a remarkable and far-reaching contribution
to Western thought, and Heidegger played a large part in
recognising this legacy.

Yet Parmenides's only known work is a single poem, of
which we have pieces: 'On Nature'. This puzzling sage, who
has challenged great scholars, left us less than a pamphlet:
two leaves, in my edition. Passages are missing, blocks of
text have migrated, and centuries of copying and recopying
have introduced errors: a letter here, a suffix there. Alongside
these often banal mistakes, the surviving verses are in Ionic
Greek—it is a work of translation, and so of ambiguity. And
many of Parmenides's ideas were paraphrased in light of later
philosophies—those of Plato and Aristotle, for example. So
the fragments we receive have been read for centuries in light
of borrowed auras.

Because they are fractured in this way, Parmenides's enigmatic scraps encourage curiosity. History, archaeology, linguistics, anthropology, literary criticism, philosophy—the modern researcher uses specialist study to fill in the gaps. Of course, scholarship can illuminate everything from Coleridge's 'Kubla Khan' to Frank Miller's Batman. But the Presocratics make this invitation more obvious: like a pottery shard, the broken bits ask for careful restoration. Parmenides appeals to the inquisitive reader, who takes pleasure in searching for possibilities beyond the page.

THE JUMP

Heidegger typified this probing outlook, complaining that 'crude' and 'un-Greek' translations missed the point. In *An Introduction to Metaphysics*, lectures delivered during the 1930s at the University of Freiburg, he argued that Western philosophy has been a continual and tragic misinterpretation of Presocratic wisdom. We must read Parmenides, he said, not as an eighteenth-century German, but as a fifth-century Greek. In particular, Heidegger took one of Parmenides's phrases and interpreted it anew: 'thinking and being are the same'.

For Heidegger, the usual translation of this line was bunkum. The ancient Greek did not mean cogitation was the same as existence; that thought simply *is* reality. He meant that thinking and being belong together. Thinking, or *noein* in Greek, is a receptive orientation to being; and being, *physis*, is a movement that rises up to meet us. To be human, Heidegger said, is to receive being in some way: as Plato's forms, Aristotle's substance, Christianity's God, and so on. Every era has its own way of greeting being. But this only happens because we are uniquely in and of being in the first place; because we are able to reveal reality as one thing or another. In fact, we are these revelations of being: a brief clearing in an otherwise dark forest.

So Heidegger read Parmenides as part of a lost beginning. He wanted to show how sensitive the Presocratics were to the question of being. They saw it, not as a definite idea or thing, but as a plenum of possibility. They were governed by 'astonishment', he argued in *What is Philosophy?* After Plato, being was interpreted as some definite something: an ideal form, fungible stuff, or deductive fact. It lost its rich openness and became totally humanised—what Heidegger called 'metaphysics'. Heidegger also argued that this amnesia about being was behind the worst of modern civilisation: war, technological alienation, even Nazism. Common to industrial agriculture, atomic bombs and gas chambers is *Gestell*: the world and ourselves as a collection of stuff to be controlled. For Heidegger, this was the essence of technology, bringing with it 'the darkening of the world, the flight of the gods'. After Parmenides: the fall.

This précis misses the sophistication of Heidegger's work, as well as its maddeningly haughty vagueness. It passes over his provocative ideas about truth, language and art, which I discuss elsewhere. And I am silent for now on the persuasiveness of Heidegger's vision: tying cultural criticism to a history of ontology. More revealing for curiosity is how the German philosopher interpreted Parmenides anew.

In *Introduction to Metaphysics*, Heidegger reflected briefly on his take on the Presocratics. He was aware of its strangeness, and recognised that it seemed absurd and whimsical. To most, it looked like a 'farfetched and one-sided Heideggerian exegesis', he wrote, fully realising the mockery it brought. Heidegger even admitted that his analysis lacked certainty;

that it was more a 'jump' than the usual academic plodding along well-trod paths. Almost forty years after writing this, he gave a seminar on a Parmenides phrase: 'the well-rounded, unshaking heart of truth'. There, Heidegger said that his interpretation seemed 'unprovable', but only to those without authentic Greek thinking.

Yet for all his talk of primordial origins, Heidegger was developing a particularly modern, German philosophy. It was informed by his mentor Edmund Husserl, who in turn was responding to the legacy of Immanuel Kant. As Heidegger himself confessed in his autobiographical reflections, there were concepts and themes that goaded him right from the beginning. His career was also marked by his provincial Catholic childhood, Protestant theology, anti-Enlightenment Romanticism, and by Germany's politics between the wars. Most saddeningly, in the Presocratics Heidegger saw the chance for a German renewal, which he identified with 'the inner truth and greatness' of Nazism. He also discovered in these ancient thinkers a way to avoid considering the Third Reich's horrific consequences, and his part in the regime. From this rare perspective of pure existence, the stuff of ordinary life—contentment and suffering, democracy and fascism, creativity and exploitation—seems very far away. These profound but aloof works played a role in what historian Richard Wolin calls 'Heidegger's personal strategy of denial.'

So the German philosopher certainly looked for new possibilities in Parmenides—yet they were typically Martin Heidegger's, not those of the Presocratics. For half a century, the 'secret king' of the Black Forest told a similar story about Western civilisation's decline: we forgot the basic question of existence. What he discovered in Parmenides was his own answer to this question. Elsewhere, Heidegger acknowledged the 'violence' of his reading, and reportedly said that his study of Kant was dodgy Kant but excellent Heidegger. There is nothing wrong with interpreting inventively; no vice in riffing off another author's suggestive words. But Heidegger advertised *Introduction to Metaphysics*, and many other later works, as a faithful record of ancient Greek wisdom, and an explanation of the world's crises. And he did so with a tone of superiority at odds with the scant evidence he cited.

If curiosity like Borges's resists the inertia of being, Heidegger's was a characteristic rejection of stubborn facts altogether. The achievements of Parmenides were put aside in favour of novel speculation; very personal possibilities triumphed over the actual.

None of this erases Heidegger's philosophical achievements. He was a potent thinker, who informed and often inspired countless thinkers—myself included. He was, in his way, profoundly curious. His analyses demonstrate a hunter's resolve, and not simply in his rustic kitsch ('this philosophical work … belongs right in the middle of the peasants' work'). Heidegger chased linguistic histories, sniffed out obscure connotations, spied the play of reason over millennia. This was a powerful mind, exercising itself. In Heidegger's lectures and treatises, there is the pleasure Hume saw in hunting and philosophy: 'the motion, the attention, the difficulty, and the uncertainty'. Heidegger himself scorned curiosity in *Being and Time*, but only of an idle sort: distraction from basic questions of existence. In his Parmenides readings, Heidegger revealed a passionate interest in textual possibilities, hidden or forgotten for centuries. And in doing so, he offered a more profound theory of possibility itself: part of being's basic plenitude.

But as a reader, Heidegger had his own manias. It is no coincidence that the philosopher found these in Parmenides' four pages: he put them there. 'Whoever thinks envisions possibilities,' wrote philosopher Hans-Georg Gadamer of Heidegger's Nazism. 'Whoever envisions possibilities with great clarity may also see what he wants to see—which may not actually exist at all.' The same was true of the professor's interpretation of Parmenides. In the infinite library, Martin Heidegger kept borrowing volumes by Martin Heidegger.

CURIOUS ABOUT CURIOSITY

This adventurous forgetting is more common with scholars. The urge to move beyond the page estranges us from the work. We chase the next illuminating 'maybe', losing sight of the words we began with.

The problem is not iconoclastic interpretation; not disorienting or disturbing responses—this is all the stuff of creative reading. 'There is a joy in getting someone to hand us *their* butterfly,' quipped novelist Zadie Smith, 'so we can spend twenty pages making the case for its being *our* giraffe.' The problem is confusing these creations with the author's achievements. We need not bow meekly to a writer's motives or purposes, particularly when these are lost or obscure. But it is revealing and fair to recognise an author's choices where we can. As Russian philosopher and literary theorist Mikhail Bakhtin argued, we cannot hold a writer responsible for their milieu. But we can try to be clear about their decisions within it. We note these phrases, this rhythm, that structure, those themes. We invent the author through the text, but not randomly or capriciously. 'We imagine to ourselves,' as Bakhtin put it, 'what the speaker wishes to say.' Curiosity turns monstrous when it no longer respects this, the 'will' of the author.

With academics, this mistake is often part of what Bourdieu called the 'scholastic disposition'. The scholar takes for granted the conditions of his own work. He forgets not only the money behind his leisure and power behind his pronouncements, but also the training behind his thinking—the scholar 'credits agents with his own vision', as Bourdieu put it. Sociologists and anthropologists, for example, see their own abstractions in the communities they study. Likewise, Heidegger saw modern German ontology in ancient Greeks.

If intellectuals like Heidegger are more prone to over-reaching, the basic tendency is more common. This is not a failure of scrutiny, but of its focus: when curiosity is not sufficiently conscious of its own motives. Curiosity is best when it looks back at itself, questioning its own interrogations.

Take Batman, who snatched my consciousness as a misanthropic teenager. Clearly the Gotham mythos continues to hold my focus as an adult. I am drawn to the Dark Knight world for its pathos and thrills, but also for its cultural power: the glimpses it gives of contemporary society. Batman is neither singular nor static. There are precursors and variations. And I can read these stories, weekly if need be, for fun and intellectual exercise. However challenging the historical fact-finding or symbolic analysis might be, it is existentially easy to read Batman. Less simple is this curiosity, directed against curiosity: the drives behind my own interest.

As a child, I was drawn to Batman for his righteous rage and victorious perseverance—classic petty wish fulfilment. But looking back now, there was another longing: for truth. *Death in the Family*, which features the murder of Robin by the Joker, felt like an initiation. The villain beats the young sidekick with a crowbar, then blows him up. I will never forget the unsettlingly colourful panels: huge, red-lipped grin against white skin, purple steel arcing over and over, silhouetted by a bright orange backdrop. The clown won, and this was primally satisfying. Not because I wanted the boy to die, or because I sympathised with the criminal. I believed I was confronting stark existence: madness, death, grief. The mocking destruction of vivacious youth, so rarely seen in children's literature. The tone of these issues, for all their epic superheroism, was pessimistic. In an earlier scene, Batman and Robin question Lady Shiva, whom they believe is the Boy Wonder's lost mother. First, she laughingly suggests she cannot know. 'I've dropped litters,' she sneers, 'in every corner of the globe!' Then, injected with a truth drug, she confesses: she is childless. Her slurred 'no' changes the atmosphere entirely, from swaggering antagonism to quiet confession. Again, this seemed revelatory. I was witnessing not only a neatly tragic plot, but also a moment of mature reckoning: a soldier exposing her life unlived. To me, this was recompense for years of social distance. Batman afforded the conceit of adult wisdom, gained one panel at a time.

And now? As the nods to Batman suggest, perhaps this need for recognition continues, only in the form of scholarly strutting. By waving aside the curtains between high and low culture, Heidegger and superheroes, I display my rejection of academic stuffiness. I reveal youthfulness and mainstream relevance, and invest in the symbolic capital of the hip intellectual. A casual geek among university staff, and highfaluting philosopher among lay nerds, I seek singularity in each subculture. Alongside this Žižek move, I reveal the universal aspirations of philosophy; the confidence to cross the borders of genres, disciplines, epochs, without concern for my academic passport.

This does not make my readings of Borges, Batman or Heidegger false. It simply suggests that my scholarship need not be pure; that there are less congenial drives alongside the pleasure of cognitive effort. Curiosity about curiosity unmasks its own mixed humanity.

PATIENCE

Boredom at Buckingham Palace

It is teatime. Her Majesty Queen Elizabeth II is reading a novel. Every so often, she makes notes with a pencil. Then suddenly the silence is cracked: 'Oh, do get on,' she says. The Queen is not scolding the maid (who apologises anyway), but the author: Henry James, master of Victorian fiction.

Part of the wit in this scene, from Alan Bennett's novella *The Uncommon Reader*, is the very fact of Her Majesty's involvement with James. Bennett's Queen is a no-nonsense matriarch, raised to privilege but also to duty. She is not a reader: that is, someone who identifies with the world of wordy but quiet withdrawal. She only begins her literary adventure because one of her corgis flees into a travelling library. Out of embarrassment, the Queen of England borrows a novel by Ivy Compton-Burnett, by now well out of fashion. This is a bit 'duff', but the next volume is just right: *The Pursuit of*

Love by Nancy Mitford. Mitford's prose is known for its easy sparkle—'one races on chuckling from page to page', wrote Evelyn Waugh, 'without noticing the solid structure'. And Mitford has the right aristocratic connections. The Queen is taken in, and slowly the ribbon-snipper is pulled away from public responsibility, towards the strange luxury of art. Bennett's portrayal of the monarch, caught between vocation and exploration, is both charming and moving.

But Her Majesty's outburst at Henry James is more than a comedic juxtaposition of regal and bourgeois literary worlds. It is more universal. Bennett's portrait invites laughter because the Queen's haste is so familiar: groaning at meandering prose or drawn-out plotting is part of the reader's lot.

LEVIATHAN

Henry James is arguably the king of circumlocution. In late novels like *The Golden Bowl*, his sentences swell and throb and, only after great straining over many finicky lines, finally pop. This is combined with an interest in psychological subtlety instead of overt drama—James's canvas is often consciousness itself. For all the swaying bulk, bugger all happens. HG Wells, the novelist's younger contemporary, wrote of James's later novels as 'leviathan retrieving pebbles'.

Take these lines from *The Golden Bowl*, as the heroine's husband Prince Amerigo and friend Charlotte look for a wedding present:

> The man in the little shop in which, well after this, they lingered longest, the small but interesting dealer in the Bloomsbury street who was remarkable for an insistence not importunate, inasmuch as it was

> mainly mute, but singularly, intensely coercive—this
> personage fixed on his visitors an extraordinary pair
> of eyes and looked from one to the other while they
> considered the object with which he appeared mainly
> to hope to tempt them.

This is *one sentence*. Not as long as part of Molly Bloom's soliloquy in Joyce's *Ulysses*—over four thousand words—but lengthy enough, and one of many.

To be fair to the novelist, this antiques trader is vital to James's plot. The merchant tries to sell Amerigo a gilded crystal bowl with a fault, which provides a symbol for the narrative: the Prince's marriage to American Maggie Verver is also a precious thing with a subtle flaw. And this very shopping trip initiates the infidelity between Amerigo and Charlotte, which almost cracks the marriage. The trader also witnesses this drama's flirty beginnings, and his quiet fervour adds to the atmosphere of transgression. So in portraying the dealer, James is not painting idly.

But the prose itself is agonisingly protracted: clauses within clauses, commas and em dashes, constantly deferring the full stop. Likewise for the stories themselves. After *The Golden Bowl* was published, Henry's brother, philosopher and psychologist William James, asked him to write a new novel 'with no twilight or mustiness … and absolute straightness in the style'. (Surprise: Henry did not.) In his language and narrative, Henry James inches forward, writing everything but the point. Yes, he gets there in the end. The kiss between Isabel Archer and Caspar Goodwood in *The Portrait of a Lady* is an orgasm only barely contained by etiquette. 'His kiss was like white lightning, a flash that spread, and spread again, and stayed,' James wrote, 'and it was extraordinarily as if, while she took it, she felt each thing in his hard manhood that least pleased her.' But to reach this climax takes many hours of whispering and fumbling in the literary back seat.

For Her Majesty, this slow evasiveness is a problem. Coming to literature in her late seventies, she is aware of her mortality. 'For the first time in her life,' wrote Bennett, 'she felt there was a great deal she had missed.' This recognition drives the Queen to read widely, but also hurriedly. There are so many books, and so few years: devoting another minute to Jamesian prose seems profligate.

YAWNING IN THE SADDLE-BAG

Central to the Queen's frustration is the discomfort of tedium: reading James, she feels time is being wasted. She is aware of the seconds passing, and of their relation to her past and future. She recalls promising beginnings, and hopes for some quick denouement. And just as importantly, she brings along her regrets and sorrows, while also reaching out towards her own death. ('At her age, people thought, why bother?')

This familiar feeling is intimately connected to temporality; to the way in which we construct time. It is easy to perceive temporality as just a series of points: the marks on an analogue face, the digits on a wristwatch. No doubt these are essential—the contrivances that synchronise a planet. This is what enables the Queen and Duke to wave grumpily from their carriage, speeding up 'to pick up the two minutes that have been lost' (because Her Majesty forgot her novel). It is impossible to make sense of modern life without recognising clock time and its continually increasing precision. But there is no one time—there are *times*. Corgis and roses, palace staff and schools, the City and Balmoral—each has its own rhythms, cycles and shifts. Clock time dominates, but its neat ubiquity is partly an illusion. What allows the Queen to wave reliably from The Mall, then fly punctually to Wales for visits, is a global system of coordination that can obscure her distinctive human time.

In *Psychology: The Briefer Course*, Henry James's disapproving brother William argued that there is no single second, cut off from its fellows. This is an abstraction, which fractures the more basic advance of human time. For us, temporality is a continual process of creation: a reaching, groping and throwing of the self, forward and back. William wrote that we all sit on a 'saddle-bag of time': astride the present, looking back to the past and forward to the future. The first is reconstructed in memory, the second is just constructed, and both play upon the 'now'. The clock's ticks, or even our own feel for the current moment, emerge from a more basic temporality—what William called a 'duration'.

This is essential to reading, since every word joins its remembered ancestors and imagined descendants. It is because we recall previous paragraphs, and anticipate new ones, that the current phrases make sense. It is because she learns about the Prince's waywardness in the beginning of *The Golden Bowl* that the Queen can envisage his later deception and subtle defeat. 'We seem to feel the interval of time as a whole,' William wrote, 'with its two ends embedded in it.'

This distinctive human time also illuminates boredom. While reading Henry James, Her Majesty is more conscious of time's passing because she is *not* fully committed to the novel. Her mind is actually on itself, busy dividing life into past, present and future. This is what gives the Queen the unique discomfort of tedium: the dull succession of what William James called 'empty time'. Instead of committing herself to the text, she is confronting her own mental vacuity. 'A day full of waiting,' wrote William, 'will seem a small eternity.' The Queen, as she sips her afternoon Darjeeling and struggles with Jamesian prose, is unhappily aware of this infinity—knowing full well that such days are actually numbered. 'Far from wanting time to pass,' she says, 'one just wishes one had more of it.'

The effort to finish a work, then, is only partly imaginative: turning letters into worlds. It is also the labour required when this fails; when perception confronts itself, instead of turning to the inventions that let hours recede. Continuing with an author like Henry James, from first to last lines, is less an exercise in sociability and more a confrontation with oneself. Not the whole 'I', with its amusing idiosyncrasies, but the impersonal automaton that marks off moments. This meeting can also have an awkward existential consequence: the anguish of mortality, as the sequence of 'now' suggests its end. *The Uncommon Reader* reveals that reading can be painful because it makes us endure the very human feeling of time running out.

WAITING TO BE TENDERISED

This discomfort, epitomised by Bennett's Elizabeth II, highlights the need for patience when reading. Unlike courage or justice, this virtue has received few classical philosophical and theological treatments. Plato praised perseverance in his *Republic*, writing that 'we plume ourselves ... on our ability to remain calm and endure'. But this is more about manly restraint than patience proper. Aristotle barely touched on it in *Nicomachean Ethics*, instead discussing the 'servility' of those who suffer without anger. Thomas Aquinas, in his

Summa Theologica, lauded patience, but only briefly and with more plaudits for love and grace. It is Augustine who gave the fullest account, in 'On Patience', but this treatise is more about spiritual forbearance than Her Majesty's willingness to put up with high Victorian phrasing.

Still, there is a broad consensus: patience is about bearing ills, rather than confronting horrors—it is not bravery, in other words. To be patient is to tolerate physical pain or what Augustine called 'adversities or filthiness of things or words'. With Her Majesty, what is 'tedious to rehearse', as Augustine put it, is the ticking of her own mental clock, which is highlighted by James's prose.

Boredom is not the sole literary pain, of course. Taking only Henry James as an example, there is the uneasiness of Isabel's decline in *The Portrait of a Lady*; witnessing the waste as freedom, fearing itself, embraces malicious security. There is the wince as James presents Strether in *The Ambassadors* as a human warning: 'Live all you can'. There is the aesthetic displeasure as James rolls out a clumsy phrase: 'I had a mystic prescience of how fond of the murky modern Babylon I was one day to become'. This line, from his marvellous travel essay 'London', is not monotonous but simply ugly. By offering experiences, text also evokes emotions, and these can be everything from annoyance to eviscerating anguish. As James noted in the preface to *The Portrait of a Lady*, there are infinite windows in the 'house of fiction', and each view can occasion some torment. Likewise for poetry and drama, philosophy and history. Sometimes we suffer because the author has failed, and sometimes because she has not; because her words rightly prompt misery or fury. Tedium is one of the many pikes assembled around text—to mount the walls is to risk puncture.

This is why endurance is cultivated: not simply for its own sake, but for some worthwhile end. For Aquinas and Augustine, patience is a virtue because the saint or martyr is hurt for salvation's sake: 'true patience of the righteous', as Augustine put it, 'from which is in them the love of God'. Clearly the Queen will not find redemption in *The Golden Bowl*, a tale of adultery and worldly marriage. But the point is clear enough: forbearance is valuable because it contributes to something good—otherwise it is simply stubbornness or numbness. Cicero's definition, in his *De Inventione*, is typically concise: 'Patience is a voluntary and sustained endurance, for the sake of what is honourable or advantageous, of difficult and painful labours'. So getting to the final flyleaf is important because reading the whole text offers something otherwise unobtainable.

For Bennett's Queen, novels are always completed because she was raised with a sense of duty. 'Books, bread and butter, mashed potato—one finishes what's on one's plate,' she tells the librarian. This is not a virtue, since it is a rule, and a clumsy one at that. But there is another reason for her diligence, which Bennett slowly reveals: fiction is an invitation to consider other minds, and to feel more keenly their troubles. After she chastises Henry James, and the maid mistakenly apologises, Elizabeth II calls out: 'Not you, Alice'. This is a noteworthy change, as normally she is aloof to others. Literature, she reflects, is encouraging her to be more sympathetic. This does not mean the Queen is less authoritative: she still carries herself with the loftiness of her state. Yet her regal command is softened by an awareness of foreign feelings. 'At the risk of sounding like a piece of steak,' she says of books, 'they tenderise one.' Bennett reveals the slow transformation from 'me' to 'we', which arises when the reader is invited to imagine another's consciousness. Her Majesty's patience is rewarded with a more abraded psyche—this is Cicero's 'honourable or advantageous' recompense.

The message of the Queen's literary edification is not that every work worth completing is an emotional schooling. A sometimes tedious book can have various benefits. Aristotle's *Nicomachean Ethics* has passages of epic density ('things are called good both in the category of substance and in that of quality and in that of relation, and that which is *per se* …'). But I finish reading the lectures with greater intellectual precision. In Dante's *Paradiso*, I slog through hundreds of theological stanzas, letters blurred by my tiredness. Yet in the end, I welcome the poet's supernatural architecture and revelation of cosmic charity: 'my will and my desire, like wheels revolving / with an even motion, were turning with / the Love that moves the Sun and all the other stars'. In each case, there are moments when I am more aware of my own boredom than I am of the words; when tedium replaces curiosity or exultation. I suffer the pulses of my own recoiling consciousness. The same might be said for the pessimistic grandeur of *Moby-Dick* or Batman's quiet grief in *Flashpoint*. On some pages I am just counting the seconds, yet the recompense is worth the investment: the 'shining moment', as novelist and critic Delia Falconer put it, that joins others to fluoresce in memory. Patience is knowing this price and, like Her grumbling Majesty, having the determination to pay it.

Literary patience is not a duty to read every work to the end; to endure a thousand smug tweets or stanzas of doggerel. What constitutes patience changes with text and reader. Despite his fussy prose, Henry James actually makes patience easier, as literary reimbursement is likely. For all the criticism of his Victorian language, the Master is rightly praised for his psychological acumen and aesthetic ambition. Virginia Woolf, reviewing James's letters, wrote of the 'enormous, sustained, increasing, and overwhelming love of life' that suffuses his words. Critics will quarrel about the Master's merits in this novel or that short story, but his oeuvre is well respected. The Queen is right to persevere.

This is not to say that I *ought* to enjoy James's work. I might be in the mood for a dumb thriller or brutal poem; might be too restless for 'The Figure in the Carpet' or, perhaps following Her Majesty, too tired by teatime for a work like *The Golden Bowl*. James's work demonstrates rare talent and merits some forbearance—just not every day, for every reader. There is no ethical command to pick up his work, or that of any other prolix author. But if I am in the right humour, patience will help me welcome whatever is proffered.

PUTTING DOWN DAN BROWN

Patience is trickier with less nuanced or ambitious authors. Someone like Dan Brown does not necessarily deserve my perseverance. Reading his *The Da Vinci Code* is a surreal business. Not because of Brown's esoteric symbols or historical mysteries, which are standard thriller props. The novel is weird because it is simultaneously easy and harrying.

What simplifies Brown's pages is the lack of innovation and sympathy: the prose is almost wholly cliché and the characters rice-paper puppets. *The Da Vinci Code* is pure plot, without the complications of Henry James's language or psychological nuance. It takes zero toil to move from scene to scene, puzzle to puzzle. It is masterfully generic. Brown's bestselling story is perfect for mass audiences, with little in common but their gratitude for a brief escape.

But this is also what makes *The Da Vinci Code* a strain. From the first chapter, I cringe at the hackneyed metaphors, which have no particular signature of authorship. The 'heavy fist pounded'. Toes 'sink deep' into a carpet. Of course, a bathrobe is 'donned'. These familiar verbs and adjectives are the equivalent of a grown-up lullaby: sung every day, consolingly, for generations. His hero, Robert Langdon, is a persona. I never get past the mask into a mind. The only player with some psychological subtlety is Silas, the masochistic albino priest. Because Brown's prose is so commonplace, his characters so transparent, I keep stopping every few sentences. What might be frictionless entertainment is ruined by my need for some psychological abrasion; for the 'tenderising' discovered by Bennett's Queen. *The Da Vinci Code* is *for* humans but not about them, and this mars the smooth plotting. I want the novel to end—not for the climax, but for the banality to stop.

In this light, patience depends not only on the work, but also on why I am reading it. It takes no forbearance to enjoy *The Da Vinci Code* as an anodyne. It is an exemplary page-turner, which easily passes the time. Yet if I am reading Brown's prose as a research exercise, it hurts. His phrasing and characterisation leave me uncomfortably aware of my mortality. 'Your enjoyment will eventually depend,' wrote Clive James about Brown's *Inferno* in *Prospect*, 'on how much you … can revel in the task of decoding the text to lay bare the full extent to which the author can't write.' The same is true of *The Da Vinci Code*. And finishing Brown's novel for its scientific and historical facts is not patient at all, since experts regard it as bunkum. This is not quite Aristotle's 'servility', or slowness of anger, but it is close: a willingness to suffer, pointlessly.

Henry James understood this. In *The Golden Bowl*, the Prince tells his old lover: 'It's precisely boring oneself without relief … that takes courage'. His conceit is simple: by keeping up the façade of a good husband and son-in-law, he preserves the freedom to cheat. But the Prince is deceiving himself. At best, this is not courage but selfish persistence. The noble puts up with droning company for his own private thrills. True forbearance would prompt Amerigo to salvage his marriage, or at least end it.

Likewise, a patient reader might pick up a Dan Brown novel for subtle prose, psychological acumen or scholarly erudition—then rightly put it down soon after, permanently.

WORTH GRUMBLING FOR

Patience is not a sexy virtue, but it is prized because the benefits of reading are never instantaneous. It is only through specific, successive phrases that the author's ideas, moods, stories can be invented; that arguments or sufferings can be recreated. Isabel Archer's kiss makes no sense without the pussyfooting that precedes it.

By allowing them to press on past the point of comfort, forbearance can leave readers with greater awareness of themselves: recognition of sympathies or animating concepts. In his sly short story 'The Story in It', James described a bored reader who 'has asked for bread and been given a stone'. But as James himself noted, part of becoming a discerning reader is recognising that the stone is in fact grain: it simply takes a little art to make it edible. *The Golden Bowl* is a slog, but the finale involves one of the finest descriptions of adult maturation in English. To reach these vistas, readers may have to endure a less edifying view: the vacant cadence of their own minds, as attention dims.

This can become easier. Audiences can become slowly accustomed to circumlocution and stretched storytelling. Preparing for *The Golden Bowl* might include beginning with James's short stories and working up through *The Europeans* to *The Portrait of a Lady*. Tales like 'The Figure in the Carpet' and *The Aspern Papers* are intricate works, which offer the Master's atmosphere in miniature: the hothouse of social exotics, pruning and picking one another. William James slighted *The Europeans* as a 'thin' novel, and his brother cautiously agreed. Yet it provides a memorable portrait of the New England society Henry left behind, and foreshadows many classic Jamesian themes: old against new world, happiness forsaken for familiarity, the ache of liberty. These works cannot be reduced to literary training wheels, to be unbolted and tossed once balance is achieved. They are worth enjoying for themselves. But they can also broaden and deepen our capacity for pleasure—or at least comprehension. Similarly, it is easier to cleave to Aristotle after Plato and, in some ways, Dante after Aquinas. Not because the first authors are simplistic, but because they helped to create the materials from which the later masterworks were wrought. They are introductions to a certain community of problems, or conception of the universe. Progenitors, not primers.

Alongside this cultivation, it is vital to decide why becoming more patient is worthwhile in the first place. There are many reasons for reading, from mere preoccupation, to heightened sympathy, to conceptual clarity, to sublime revelation. We can pass time with HG Wells or explore it with Marcel Proust. Becoming confused about these ends might be a pleasant surprise—looking for Edwardian thrills and finding impressionistic nostalgia. But these mistakes can also be narrowing, because they distort the worth of sophisticated literature. We are animals of easy torpor, and it takes little time for choices to become obvious givens; for the polish of the familiar to outshine novelty. Habits become their own justifications, and it becomes increasingly more difficult to imagine the other genres, styles, themes and characters—let alone their rewards. This is the danger of Dan Brown and his bubblegum peers: not that they are trivial, but that they can become a schooling in numbed haste. They allow us to ignore why authors like Henry James are worth grumbling for. We are not amused.

HOW COULD YOU KNOW?

Alan Bennett's Queen is anxious about mortality, fearing that life will be completed well before the 'to read' pile. But Elizabeth II's age is also an advantage: she has maturity. Her decades have given her more to discover. Public performance and domestic squabbles, war service and political tiptoeing, youth's potential and the firm actuality of life's decline—each adds to her sensibility. Had she been a reader at twenty—before marriage, parenthood, reign and grief—Her Majesty might have dropped James altogether.

This happens to the most judicious readers. Novelist Evelyn Waugh, writing in his early forties, described the kick of a new novel by the Master. 'What an enormous, uncovenanted blessing to have kept Henry James for middle age,' he said, 'and to turn, as the door shuts behind the departing guest, to a first reading of *Portrait of a Lady*.' This was a thrill withheld and luxuriated within—something for the particular solitude of a recently vacated room. But it was a joy foreign to the younger Waugh, decades in the making.

Others try too soon. Novelist Sheila Kaye-Smith wrote of the 'conscientious' reading that spoiled her introduction to Charles Dickens. Not because she was not ready for the weeping—this came copiously, at fifteen. Kaye-Smith reflected that her laughter was childish. 'A true sense of humour is an adult quality, the gift of experience,' she wrote in *All the Books of My Life*, 'and its full maturity is attained only when we have learned to laugh at ourselves.' As with Jane Austen, the wit in Dickens is pointed, but also pointing: a finger directed at the reader, recognising her own faults.

From sentimental drama to satire, some of the finest works afford nuance invisible to youth. It is not simply that our childish palate is changed; that Jenny Diski's acridness or Marcel Proust's faint decay becomes savoury with age. It is that, before we mature, these simply do not exist in the pages. Nostalgia, regret, mockery and loss—they attach themselves to things, and are pulled along by even the most innocent words. To read with maturity is to witness a more crowded human reality.

This does not mean we transform radically with the years. As William James argued in *Psychology*, and modern studies confirm, personality rarely changes. We can alter behaviour, and reflect with independence and acuity. We are not automatons. But nor are we perfectly free sprites, vaulting circumstance and convention on a whim. William called custom the 'fly-wheel' of society, which keeps the massive contraption running. While the mechanical metaphor is clunky, the point is compelling. '[Habit] dooms us all to fight out the battle of life upon the lines of our nurture or our early choice, and to make the best of a pursuit that disagrees,' William wrote, 'because there is no other for which we are fitted, and it is too late to begin again.' The ageing Queen is still Elizabeth Windsor.

What shifts with maturity is experience, a commonplace word that dims its own distinctiveness. Experience is not simply knowledge: certainty about facts. It is not a knack for getting on, although it can contribute to this virtue—what Aristotle called *phronesis*: practical wisdom. This is partly why the philosopher argued that the young—in years or mindset— ought to avoid political studies: they are 'inexperienced in the actions that occur in life'. Experience is a cumulative perme- ability. It does not merely pass through us, but builds upon us. Sometimes in steps, sometimes in leaps; experience grows as we age. 'One has been,' says Bennett's Queen, 'very close to events.' And these have marked her perception of things.

It is a truism that age has experiences unavailable to youth. More illuminating is the observation that both cannot help this: children can no more abstract themselves into maturity than the elderly can shrug off their decades. We can make more or less of experience; we can question or accept, confront or repress. But we cannot avoid, falsify or synthesise its basic transforming force—it must be. Even when we live idly or shrink from adventure, we gain 'thickened motive and accumulated character', as Henry James put it in his *The Ambassadors* preface.

As readers, this asks for a double patience. Most obviously, we have to abide the works. As a teenager, *The Golden Bowl* would have been lost on me. Had I tolerated James's prose wanderings and recognised the subtle signs of class and status, I still would have been out of my element. Yes, I lived with marital discord—brute and subtle, direct and by proxy—but only as a child. It is one thing to witness a marriage fraying, and another to feel the strands hold or snap. Had I picked up the novel—or worse, suffered it in high school—I would have blamed the Master for my own naïveté. It would not have been patient to finish *The Golden Bowl*, only to slander it as irrelevant.

More importantly, this would have robbed me of later pleasure and revelation—like Waugh, I turn to James now with hermetic contentment. This is the less noticeable patience: with ourselves, as readers. Because we cannot fake experience, we simply have to wait. This might be weeks, because of mood: Hegel's *Lesser Logic* put aside during the insomnia of new parenthood. This might be decades, because of age: Peter Porter's 'Random Ageist Verses', shelved for its untimely prophecies ('Here is the body fearfully beautiful / The pushy you of just nineteen— / How could you know, in shin or skull, / What's dead already in the sheen?'). The written word adds to experience, but it cannot compensate for all that age smashes, loses, abrades and beautifies. Forbearance is necessary because we are partial beings, and our incompleteness varies with time. The patient reader keeps well-stocked bookcases, and lingers gladly until the shelves are emptied and scattered by their estate.

COURAGE

The Ninja of Unfinishedness

Aged eleven, I enjoyed a daily meditation: cross-legged on a black leather couch, eyes on a mandala of prose. In one hand, dice thrown onto a polished steel and glass coffee table. In the other, one of six paperbacks called 'The Way of the Tiger': an adventure series with a stalwart ninja as its hero. Starting with *Avenger!* and ending with *Inferno!*, I devoted years to these stories, with a resolve and elation missing in the classroom.

Pencilling notes on punches, throwing stars and magical rings, I was no longer a gawky child. I was the hero Avenger, master of many weapons and few words. ('My strategy is one foot in front of the other.') For hours after school, the series made me a 'lethal master of unarmed combat'. Attacking or aligning myself with a cast of fantasy tropes, I played at balance: wise but canny, kind but brutal, meditative but decisive. (Sometimes I even avoided cheating.) Given their genre, *Avenger!* and its sequels were surprisingly edifying works of wish-fulfilment.

But wish-fulfilment they were. The hero-in-black was handsome, dangerous, absurdly talented. 'You use your skill as a bringer of death to rid the world of evil-doers,' I read, 'just as all true followers of peace must.' By the fourth book, my ninja avatar was the overlord of a city and saviour of his own god. (Really.) Meanwhile, I was an awkward provincial, mumbling with girls, muffling my father's morning screams with a pillow over my ears. I turned to fantasy precisely because of this: to afford some feeling of control, enjoyed vicariously. I was hiding in make-believe.

Yet *Inferno!*, the final volume of 'The Way of the Tiger', prompted me to read with a little more courage. This was chiefly to do with the structure of the story. Each of the first five books closed with a straightforward resolution: an assassin hit with a deftly spun ninja star, a usurper sliced. 'As ... the crowd screams its adulation,' reads the end of *Usurper!*, 'you reflect that the days ahead will be a true test of your wisdom.' The message was simple and flattering: with sweat, nous and goodness, I was destined for conquest. It is a common literary conceit, in which moral excellence and perseverance produce victory—or at least dignified defeat. There is always some final clarity. But in *Inferno!*, every decision had the same denouement: stuck in a monstrous web, waiting for a spider to fang and drink me. 'Here on the seventh tier you will make a juicy morsel for the Queen of Evil,' I read, disbelieving, 'unless you can master your despair and somehow rid Orb of its darkest blight ...' Note the *somehow* and expectant ellipsis. The absence of finality was awful. I was neither winner nor loser, saviour nor martyr.

Importantly, this was not ordinary ignorance, as if I had just misread a decisive line. ('Inwardly you smile, as you discover the can of bug spray on your belt …') The conclusion was not a cheap allegory—a wannabe Buddhist tale, for example, in which the web symbolised craving and the spider suffering. And the authors had not finished with a cheap cliffhanger, designed to tantalise before the next purchase. There *was* no next purchase. It was the end—and yet maddeningly not. It perturbed me for months.

DESPERATELY SEEKING UNITY

There was a straightforward psychological reason for my discomfort. As John Dewey argued, we are creatures of rhythm. Life has cadences: expansion and contraction, inhalation and exhalation, departure and arrival. 'Human energy gathers, is released, dammed up, frustrated and victorious,' he wrote in *Art as Experience*, 'There are rhythmic beats of want and fulfillment, pulses of doing and being withheld from doing.' There is, in all these efforts, a striving towards realisation, which is pleasurable. We seek unities, the sense of having begun and finished some whole event. And this basic physiological and psychological principle is also at work in art, including literature: we look for completion. Backstory reaches out to finale, just as epilogue reaches back to prologue. This happens with sentences, as they lead semicolon by semicolon to a given stop; with chapters, as they move from premise to conclusion; with novels, as they reveal a protagonist's growth from novice to overlord. 'Art celebrates with peculiar intensity,' said Dewey, 'the moments in which the past reinforces the present and in which the future is a quickening of what now is.'

The conclusions that punctuate literature can offer a profound feeling of achievement, which Dewey described as 'fully present'. And life without this organismic beat is so intolerable, I will often insert finality into unfinishedness. As Frank Kermode noted in *The Sense of an Ending*, even the constant tick of the clock is oppressive—I have to introduce a 'tock' to give time some gratifying shape.

This is why it took a little courage to re-read *Inferno!*, knowing its unalterable ending: it hurt, psychologically speaking. The book finished, but the story did not. There was no 'fully present' moment, other than the fact of my unease. I had to kick orcs and blow darts at chthonic fiends without, as Keats put it in a famous letter to his brothers, 'irritable reaching after fact'. So the courage was not in the dice-rolling choices to slay or stay, but in the willingness to *keep* labouring without comforting resolution. Had I flinched from the anxiety: cowardice. Had I begun to revel in the pathos: foolhardiness. Bravery lay in the joyless encounter with the lack of tock.

This is important, because life always contains some measure of unfinishedness. We are born in what the poet Horace called *in medias res*: in the middle of things. We die the same way, amid breaths, seasons, manuscripts. While existence is punctuated by the birth canal and coffin, this is only observed by others. I witness neither my life's entry nor its exit, and the various stages are real but vague—adulthood scribbled upon by childhood, and youth revised by age. My body itself is a porous thing, always stuck in a to-and-fro with the world. As Alfred North Whitehead observed in *Modes of Thought*, the body is a unity (perhaps *the* unity), but its borders are 'vague in the extreme'. This is to say nothing of various abortive lurches: chapters unwritten, arguments left partial, memories half recalled. There are endings, as Dewey noted—but rarely as many as I fantasise, and never lasting. In short, incompleteness is unavoidable. Things cease, but they do not always conclude.

By re-reading *Inferno!* I was learning to put up with this inconclusive reality. And in doing so, I was confronting a world quite alien to popular culture. There was no reward other than the encounter itself, with its futility and powerlessness. Somewhere in that boy's stubborn play was a new philosophical skill: a willingness to put on hold my creaturely horror of deficiency.

TOPPLING THE INNER TYRANT

Aristotle would take issue with this idea of literary courage. He argued that only soldiers can be truly brave, because the combatant risks death willingly and knowingly, for the good of his state. Death is 'the most terrible of all things', said Aristotle, whereas reading for leisure is neither horrifying nor politically noble. For Aristotle, only my fictional Avenger was valorous, because he was offering his life to his kingdom. If I showed some pluck, it was solely metaphorical.

This is one of Aristotle's aristocratic prejudices: taking bravery from civic and domestic labours, and reserving it for warriors. Confronting mortality is a genuine virtue, but Homo sapiens cannot flourish without civilian backbone; without citizens who care for one another and themselves, and face fears to safeguard what they value. As MacIntyre noted in *After Virtue*, 'a man who genuinely cares and has not the capacity for risking harm or danger has to define himself ... as a coward'. So 'The Way of the Tiger' was a glimpse of physical valour, and a reminder of bravery in general. It represented the willingness to be distressed for some good end.

But what end? Avoiding the lust for control and con-clusiveness. Heroes like Avenger need antagonists: tyrants who rule with force or trickery. They are not simply violent or brutal—every soldier uses force. Instead, they have a mania for authority. This was certainly true of 'The Way of the Tiger' series, in which the biggest nemeses were thugs with imperial ambitions. While better stories have more nuanced scoun-drels and villains—from Dante's Odysseus in *Inferno* to Alan Moore's Ozymandias in *Watchmen*—what often characterises evil is this craving for command. The villains do not merely lead: they *rule*, or aspire to.

This governance is evil—rather than good or simply benign—because its logic is purely instrumental. Villains see all things as means to an end, and whether the thing is a sword or person is neither here nor there. And the end itself is *their* ultimate order, some vision of perfection that legitimises every vulgar abuse and subtle ruse. Sometimes this is sincerely altruistic: a leader rules for universal freedom, true happiness, the city of God, and other abstractions. Sometimes it is for glory: a generalissimo's dynastic fantasies. Either way, fellow human beings become timber and nails in a flawless blueprint. As Isaiah Berlin put it in his excellent essay 'The Pursuit of the Ideal', 'the possibility of a final solution … turns out to be an illusion; and a very dangerous one'.

Resisting tyranny, in this light, requires more than thick sinews and martial determination. It also asks for a less fanatical consciousness, which does not covet unities; which resists the appetite for completion. This demands courage well before blades are unsheathed, to endure discomposure for the sake of a more honest mind. Picking up *Inferno!*, my young self learned a lesson unattainable for Avenger, with his

straightforward missions and superhuman will. Confronted
by obscurity, I had to stifle the little oligarch inside of me.

SEEKING AMBIGUITY

Not everyone needs a ninja for this literary emancipation.
In fact, most stories in this genre provide completeness: neat
victories, trim apocalypses. One of the most popular martial
arts novels, Eric Van Lustbader's *The Ninja*, is a primer in
Eastern mysteries—but it still affords a crisp denouement with
a dead villain. And likewise for every genre, from romance, to
westerns, to thrillers. Marianne in *Sense and Sensibility* gets
her colonel; Jane Withersteen in Zane Grey's *Riders of the
Purple Sage* loses Mormons and gains a gunslinger; James
Bond gets his Blofeld.

   This unity is a ubiquitous pleasure, and not only in fiction. In his *Modes of Thought*, Alfred North Whitehead argued
that modern philosophy has a history of false finality. Scholars
have found tidy conclusions by ignoring flux, vagueness and
relatedness, in favour of 'clear and distinct sense impressions'. His point is not that these are wrong, but that they are
abstractions from a more complicated universe. It takes a certain perseverance to give up crisp facts for Whitehead's more
nuanced cosmos. (And perhaps his cosmos, with its grand
connectedness, is itself an invention.) To develop this courage, it helps to seek out ambiguous texts—works that artfully
suggest a world undone. And these have to be savoured, not
as failed entertainments, but as exercises in honesty.

   Henry James's short story 'The Figure in the Carpet' is a
masterpiece of hinted significance, with no easy conclusion.
The narrator, a young literary critic, is humiliated when his

review of a respected novelist, Vereker, is declared 'twaddle' by the author himself. The novelist then consoles him: *everyone* misses the 'little point' of his novels. All his oeuvre is threaded by this—'the very string', says Vereker, 'that my pearls are strung on!' But not one reader has discovered it. Then what is it? Vereker will not say, and laughingly tells the young man to give up. The narrator spends a month reading all the novelist's works: nothing. He has stared at the carpet, but found no figure. He tells his friend and colleague George Corvick about the author's great secret. He too is baffled—but equally manic with curiosity. Years later, George telegraphs from India: 'Eureka. Immense'. George offers his breakthrough to his fiancée Gwendolen, then dies. Without detailing every Jamesian trick, the finale brings nothing but a groping swipe of air. Vereker, George, Gwendolen—each in receipt of something wonderful that James never reveals. 'It's my *life!*' says Gwendolen, and goes no further. The narrator is left with little but 'waves of wonder and curiosity', and the poor consolation of others' misery—a condition James sneakily evokes in his audience.

A more esoteric approach is apophatic theology, the study of what divinity is *not*. In his *Mystical Theology*, Pseudo-Dionysius the Areopagite refused to reveal exactly what God is. Writing in the late fifth or early sixth century, Dionysius argued that God cannot be thought, spoken or felt. Yet the basic idea of Dionysius's philosophy is unity: exactly what we so often long for. The Father, Son and Holy Spirit are absolutely one, and this one is the goodness, origin and culmination of all things. God is perfection: not just a perfect thing, but perfection itself. But it is because of this absolute wholeness, said Dionysius, that God is beyond us. While we might use words like 'unity', 'perfection' and 'absolute', these are just our finite symbols for something infinitely greater. Dionysus suggested using language like a sculptor chipping away marble, leaving only 'the hidden statue itself in its hidden beauty'. He then lists all things God is not, including 'goodness', 'spirit', 'Godhead', and many of the other words he himself uses. The end result is that God, all fullness and light, becomes an empty darkness—what Dionysius called 'divine gloom'. This outlook is foreign to secular thinking, but Dionysius informed not only Thomas Aquinas—and so the Catholic Church—but also modern philosophers like Martin Heidegger. For atheist readers, the challenge is not only to imagine God, but also imagine him in a strange state of yes-and-no. Less of burning bushes and frog rain, and more strange simultaneity.

Arguably the most rich invitation to ambiguity is poetry. With its tension between sensuous suggestion and straightforward representation, poetry can relax a tight grip on meaning. Some works are more prosaic than others. Alexander Pope's poetry is charismatic in its rhythm, rhyme and humour. But it is readily understandable, and Pope recognised this. His words display what he called 'True Wit': 'Nature to advantage dress'd / What was oft thought, but ne'er so well express'd.' Pope wrote in verse, but he was working more with Valéry's clear glass than amber.

Near Pope in my bookshelf, but almost in another world, is modern English poet JH Prynne. While his poems vary in style, many refuse any easy interpretation. They are evocative—often overwhelmingly so. But, unlike Pope's 'Essay on Man', they cannot be translated into some definite message. Reading Prynne's 'Moon Poem', I have a sense of someone spilling over the boundaries of themselves—or hoping to. Prynne wrote: 'it really is dark and the knowledge / of the unseen is a warmth which spreads into / the level ceremony of diffusion.' The poem reflects on the fallacy of modern freedom, suggesting we are more malleable and manipulated than we believe. 'We disperse,' he continued, 'into the ether / as waves'. But my summary here is too simplistic. Prynne's poem is thick with themes—movement and stillness, individual and community, will and habit—but not one is definitive. Even if Prynne himself inserted a 'how-to' guide with each edition, the ambiguity would remain: the words surpass his intentions. (Prynne himself argued that the 'voice of the poet' is not the 'voice of the poem'.)

James, Dionysius and Prynne are notable but not alone. The point is to deliberately chase texts that challenge easy resolutions. For me, what began with stoical Avenger continued (much later, alas) with poetry, fiction and philosophy. Whether it is the haiku of Matsuo Bashō, the short stories of Jorge Luis Borges, or the treatises of Heidegger or Emmanuel Levinas, there are exercises in ambiguity, which ask me to persevere past the first awkwardness. This does not negate Dewey's unities; the creaturely rhythms I enjoy. It prompts awareness of these urges, and the agility to sidestep them when necessary. Reading can encourage a richer ideal of heroism: not simply dominating others, but governing one's own desire to govern.

A PAIR OF RAGGED CLAWS

As an adolescent, I lost my nerve. I aped Avenger's physical courage in karate classes. But as a reader I became cowardly—I craved control.

This was partly rebellion. High school struck me as rigid, superficial and—perhaps worst of all—dull. The rote learning, the jaded teachers, the atmosphere of smug conformity—literature became a burden, not a thrill. Had I read Leonard Woolf's memoir *Sowing*, his description of St Paul's Preparatory School would have been familiar: 'I am astonished … to find that the human brain could survive the desiccation, erosion, mouldiness, frustration applied to it for seven or eight hours every day called education'. I coped with this purgatory by defining myself against it. If the popular students were earnest, studious and cooperative, I was necessarily cynical, lazy and recalcitrant. I was never one of the cool rebels—this pose was beyond me. Instead, I gauchely took on the worst of both worlds: the sloth of the slackers, the alienation of the geeks.

This clumsy outsider posture corrupted my childhood pleasure: words. Novels asked for sincerity and charity, so I replied with irony and mockery. Essays required careful analysis, so I offered casual rejection. I read, but it had no existential significance. Within a few years of reading (and re-reading) *Inferno!*, I was no longer a *reader*.

What spoiled my bibliophilia was fear of commitment. If I took the works seriously, I risked more uncertainty and psychological pain. It did not help that many of the novels were foreign to the drives of a chronically furious boy, and taught with numbing inelegance. But the estrangement was chiefly my own. To devote myself to prize-winning works on the syllabus was to invest in the institutions that had rejected me. Better to stay aloof, and keep myself safe from disappointment or disparagement.

Instead of novels or poetry, I often read comics— they provided fulfilment without ambiguity. One of my subscriptions was *Ghost Rider*. The titular antihero, with his flaming skull, bullied criminals into remorse. He caused brutal thugs to scream and weep, by looking into their eyes with his 'penance stare'. Each month I ripped open the plastic mailing slip, ready for the pleasure of righteous violence. A typical narration: 'Four of the youths have felt the soul-searing torment of the ghost rider's penance stare, and the remaining two plead for mercy from one who will show them none'. It was permissible to glory in this, Ghost Rider's vigilantism, because he was only torturing villains.

Looking back at *Ghost Rider* #5, the stories were not always superficial. They often reflected on the moral dilemmas of domination, and the dubious sacrifices of revenge. But I used the comics as a means to an end: they were an escape from doubt and weakness.

The nadir of my reading came when I was seventeen, in English Literature. In retrospect, TS Eliot's poem 'The Love Song of J Alfred Prufrock' was perfect for me. I was not Eliot's Polonius, with his bald spot and visions of rolled trousers. But Prufrock spoke to my gracelessness and hesitation. 'And should I then presume?' he keeps asking, 'And how should I begin?' While Eliot's phrasing is masterful, the mood is awkward. Prufrock covets the drawing room ladies, charming and confident, and wonders how to connect. But after all his hand-wringing and gabbing, he might still fail: 'Would it have been worth while / If one, settling a pillow or throwing off a shawl, / And turning toward the window, should say: / "That is not it at all, / That is not what I meant, at all."' This was the question of my adolescence, and my answer was chiefly 'no'. The psychological stakes were too high to try. So for all my chatter, I kept silent about the issues that mattered. Like Prufrock, my worry was transformed into shame and refusal. And like Prufrock, I had Hamlet's hesitation but not his grandeur. My private portrait of myself was not unlike Eliot's famous metaphor: 'I should have been a pair of ragged claws / Scuttling across the floors of silent seas'.

Ironically, this very fear dragged me away from Eliot's poem. I sneered at his words and their classroom milieu, including my teacher: legs crossed delicately at the knees, repeating 'coffee spoons' like a monastic mantra. I clung to clichés of literary decadence. The hermetic preciousness of Eliot's style, the snobbery of his Italian epigraph (Dante), the dubious sexuality of my (married) teacher—these were false, but they enabled my rejection of the text. I distanced myself from the poem, using all the tropes of macho stoicism I had collected. I was Prufrock avoiding Prufrock, while living a Ghost Rider caricature.

Years later, as an undergraduate, 'The Love Song of J Alfred Prufrock' became one of my favourite poems. I saw myself in Eliot's lines, and this was liberating: giving elegance to a more mundane frailty. I realised that weakness was common enough. But it could be articulated with strong, sustained intellectual effort. Behind Prufrock's hesitation was Eliot's commitment. As Clive James pointed out in 'Interior Music', parts of 'Prufrock' barely seem like poetry. But this is Eliot's achievement, taking a character of verbose foolishness and speaking him with exquisite precision. It is, in James's words, 'prose whose interior workings are calculated and refined to such a high standard that they turn incandescent'. As a philosophy student revelling in undergraduate freedom, I was brave enough to read 'Prufrock' more carefully, and observe myself in light of its glow.

While 'Prufrock' was not written to loosen the disaffection of teenage boys, it might have helped me. Yet because of my general estrangement, I overestimated the danger of Eliot's poem, and literature more generally. My fear was overblown. As Aristotle pointed out, the coward is not simply frightened, but mistakenly so: afraid of benign things, horrified by mild threats, or otherwise incapacitated by terror. 'He is deficient … in feeling confidence,' Aristotle observed, 'but he is most clearly seen as exceeding in the case of pains.' I believed that reading generously, and with dedication, would hurt more than it did. In fact, I had conflated an aid with a danger, actually increasing my malaise. For all my swagger, my reading of Eliot was craven.

BAD FAITH

Cowardice in reading is rarely discussed, partly because fear is often a welcome stimulant—the accelerated heartbeat that adds zest to the evening. Novels like Clive Barker's *Weaveworld* offer moments of carefully sharpened revulsion. I read several of Barker's works as a teenager, and was often scared by his scenes of surreal filth and gore. But I was never truly put out. The dread lasted while I read, and lingered only a little after. This vicarious panic excited me, but never threatened my psychological security. There was no courage in reading Barker, since there was no danger. Likewise for so many popular horror novels or thrillers. The fear they evoke is to be enjoyed, not overcome.

So to be craven is not to avoid bloody or eerie tales, but to read in a way that shirks risk. It might be lambasting a poem like 'Prufrock', which admits uncertainty. It might be avoiding a narrative theme that touches on some personal tragedy: domestic trauma in *What Maisie Knew* by Henry James, death of a partner in AS Byatt's *Still Life*, or banal failure to thrive in Charlotte Wood's *Animal People*. It might be trivialising a thesis, like Heidegger's *Being and Time*, which white-ants the foundations of rational individualism. The point is that timidity is something each reader cultivates and discovers for herself. It depends on what most prompts angst. The coward refuses to pick up what truly terrifies or, more craftily, refuses to imagine the frightful things at all. It is a kind of literary repression.

Cowardly reading can be what Jean-Paul Sartre called 'bad faith'. In *Being and Nothingness*, Sartre argued against the traditional idea of repression, derived from Freud. In this older outlook, the reader has a hidden drive to avoid some truth, of which his waking mind is wholly ignorant. For example, I found Eliot's depiction of silent frustration too emotionally threatening. But this urge, said the Freudian theory, was barely mine—it belonged instead to some shadowy other me, the unconscious. In reply, Sartre pointed out that I have to know *exactly* what discomfiting thing I am vetoing, in order to shut it out. And I have to know I am banning the thought, so I can deny this too. 'The censor must choose,' Sartre wrote, 'and in order to choose must be aware of so doing.' This is bad faith, because I am denying myself: not simply what I am, but my own liberty to be otherwise. Sartre gave consciousness too much transparency, but his view of repression makes sense of literary spinelessness. This was certainly my fantasy: I was neither Prufrock, nor the boy denying he was Prufrock. The timid reader not only disavows unsettling truths, but also repudiates some freedom. The words on the page are mocked, savaged or simply ignored, because this is less frightening than existential culpability.

Cowardly reading is more than a missed opportunity for comprehension; a squandered snatch of mood or notion. It is also a chance to reflect on psychological canniness: catching a cringing mind in the act, as it pretends not to know itself.

PRIDE

Gospel Untruths

White cotton shirt clinging to his bones, thinning hair combed back, Nikos Kazantzakis was hunched over his manuscript. His hand moved too slowly for his mind, warping the Greek script. Eleni, his wife, joked about this 'new personal stenography'. While alert to the charms of Antibes—'the sea smells like ripe fruit'—Kazantzakis was not on holiday. Unwilling to abide nationalist, right-wing Greece, and unable to visit America, he was working zealously in Mediterranean France. His novel was a modern retelling of the Christian Passion. 'I am so deeply immersed in the joy and agony of *The Last Temptation* that I can't lift my head,' he told his friend Börje Knös in June 1951. 'The moons get bright and fade away like lightning.'

Kazantzakis had a personal stake in the gospel story. He identified with what he called 'the dual substance of Christ':

flesh and spirit in conflict, and all the antinomies this suggests. Destruction and conservation, activity and passivity, revolution and reaction—Jesus was all these things for Kazantzakis, and a symbol of innovation. This creative urge was his daily credo, and Christ one of its exemplars. While writing this novel, one of his last, the author confessed to weeping as he laboured. 'I never followed Christ's bloody journey to Golgotha with such terror,' he wrote, 'such understanding and love, as during the days and nights when I wrote *The Last Temptation*.'

The premise of Kazantzakis's novel might seem absurd to many today, the private mythologising of an author caught between worlds. Certainly his Christ tale, like so many of his works, can appear outdated: high metaphysical drama, on a stage of nineteenth-century narrative style, spotlighted with blinding adjectives. But the story of *The Last Temptation*, and its reception in Greece and abroad, is a telling study in conceited reading: what is squandered when pride lapses into vanity. And Christianity in general is rich with clashing interpretations. This religious conflict reveals the scales that cover even the most earnest readers' eyes.

IN ABSENTIA

Despite its anachronisms, Kazantzakis's novel of the Passion is radical even today. It offers a vision of Christ's visceral, vulnerable humanity, and takes liberties with scripture. Kazantzakis wrote often of 'god', but this was a poetic expression of a metaphysical idea. He was more influenced by secular thinkers like Friedrich Nietzsche and Henri Bergson than by Paul the Apostle.

Yet unorthodox ideas did not make Kazantzakis irreligious. He was committed to theological questioning, once spending forty days in a remote mountain monastery. He read many Orthodox works, including the lives of saints and Byzantine mystics. *The Last Temptation* is a record, not only of aesthetic striving, but also of a life's spiritual adventure. 'I am certain that every free man who reads this book,' he wrote, 'will more than ever before, better than ever before, love Christ.' Kazantzakis was passionate, sincere and artful in his depiction of Jesus. 'This is somebody,' the Archbishop of Canterbury Rowan Williams remarked, 'who belongs within the family of Christian discourse in any number of interesting ways.'

Because of this, the novel deserved a considered response from Christian authorities. Surely, they too fought this war between carnality and ethereality, inertia and fervour, domesticity and holy fraternity? A handful of clergymen, East and West, corresponded and argued with Kazantzakis. But the most common reaction was righteous rejection. The Vatican listed *The Last Temptation* on its index of prohibited titles, and metropolitan bishops from the Orthodox Church in Greece campaigned to have Kazantzakis excommunicated. The Greek Orthodox Church of America condemned the novel as 'indecent, atheistic, and treasonable', in Kazantzakis's words. The Holy Synod of Athens wrote that it 'contains evil slander against the Godlike Person of Jesus Christ'. For these officials, *The Last Temptation* was an attack on Christianity and Greece as a nation and diaspora. By publishing this, they suggested, Kazantzakis was revealing the perversity of his soul.

The clergy gave the impression of fighting valiantly against a blasphemer, yet many of the critics had *never read the novel*. Some had picked up facts reported in *Estia*, one of Athens's conservative newspapers. But Kazantzakis' story, with its philosophical nuance and religious fervour, was alien to them. *The Last Temptation* was condemned *in absentia*.

The metropolitans who censured Kazantzakis were, to a casual observer, just doing their job. As in Catholicism, an Orthodox bishop is an *episkopos*: 'overseer'. This is no trivial duty, since ordinary Christians are not expected to care wholly for themselves. In *Acts*, Paul reveals that the church elders are custodians of their Christian communities, a role that has been preserved for almost two millennia. 'The Holy Ghost,' he says to the men of Ephesus, 'hath made you overseers'. Paul also speaks of bishops as shepherds for the faithful, and the metaphor continues throughout the gospel and theology. The logic is straightforwardly hierarchical. Bishops have more power, but also more responsibility. The same analogy is true of pastors: the words in Latin and Greek mean 'shepherd'. These men, along with other elders, have to protect the flock from what Paul calls 'grievous wolves', including other bishops 'speaking perverse things'.

So the problem with the condemnation of *The Last Temptation* is not that the clergy were protecting Christians— this was business as usual. The problem is that they could not defend the faithful against a novel they had not read. Since they never braved the prose itself, almost everything horrifying about *The Last Temptation* came from them. Every 'sacrilege' against Christ, perversion of the Passion, and mockery of the gospel was invented by these clergymen. In this, they failed as Christian overseers. To continue with their own traditional metaphor, a shepherd ought to actually know the threat is a wolf and not a sheepdog. Not having read *The Last Temptation*, they were ignorant of its dangers; of the direction in which its teeth were bared. By attacking the novelist, the priests also refused to recognise what was monstrous in themselves: the horrors they imagined, all on their own.

THE DOWNFALL OF ME

The word for the clergy's failing is vanity, or what is often translated as conceit, arrogance or 'overweening pride'. As David Hume pointed out in his *A Treatise of Human Nature*, pride is pleasure in my own achievements: the joy that comes from some beautiful or good thing, which is *mine*. In Aristotle's typically pagan outlook, pride is psychologically and socially helpful, nudging citizens to strive and rewarding them for their sacrifices. Proud men are gratified by their needful deeds. But those who wrongfully claim glories are, in Aristotle's words, 'fools and ignorant of themselves'. His portrayal of this conceit is lightly comedic: vain men put on airs and 'adorn themselves with clothing and outward show', but they are soon discovered. Vanity is not only deluded, but also ridiculous.

What was a vice for the Greeks was a sin for the church fathers, who celebrated meekness. Paul tells the Ephesians that he is 'serving the Lord with all humility of mind'. (Granted, it takes a certain kind of modesty to take responsibility for the salvation of humanity.) For Paul and later theologians like Augustine, the spirit of Christ cannot enter the soul of an arrogant overseer. And importantly, this applies to scholarship. 'God has certainly filled my head with a great many thoughts,' wrote Ignatius of Antioch in the first century, 'but I am careful of my own limitations, for fear boasting should be the downfall of me.' For the Christian fathers, crowing about literary study was bad enough—*falsely* implying knowledge, as the Orthodox clergy did with Kazantzakis's novel, was wickedly vain.

Despite their conflicts, the Christian and pagan thinkers have a common suspicion of vanity: it is covetous and deluded. For Aristotle, the conceited citizen advertises his great deeds—but he never does them. For theologians, the arrogant Christian glories in his own charity or faith, without recognising these as God's gifts. In each case, the poseur tries to protect a pleasing idea of himself, and genuine excellence leaves him feeling monstrous or weak.

This vanity can become chronic. As his egotism grows, so does the braggart's delusion. Sick with what Paul in *Ephesians* calls blindness of heart, he embroiders himself with others' success and cuts ties with his own failures—and does both with increasing ferocity. 'A fool must always find some person that is more foolish,' wrote Hume, 'in order to keep himself in good humour with his own parts and understanding.' And when suitable fools cannot be found, they are invented.

This is exactly what happens with conceited reading—or *not* reading. The Orthodox clergy were fluffing themselves with Kazantzakis. Not only by faking familiarity with *The Last Temptation*, but also by conjuring up a demon to attack: a blasphemer against whom they looked more righteous. This was a way to doll up their institutional façade—a fact that Kazantzakis recognised when he challenged his critics' morality. 'I pray that your conscience,' he wrote, 'may be as clear as mine.'

No doubt similar vanity occurs in all cults and ideologies. The common mistake is neither worship nor supernaturalism, but *necessarily* ignorant authority. Threatened by irrelevance or impotence, a pundit saves face by bluffing mastery. This not only patches up their persona, but also hides their adversaries' nuance, making conflict easier. Those with weak identities need simple enemies. But for community leaders, this deceit also makes their pretend eminence dangerous: careless readers are poor shepherds.

HATE READERS

Because much of its strife is scriptural, theology can make the symptoms of literary vanity easier to spot. Authors like Augustine and Aquinas also provide sharp ethical instruments to treat the malaise.

But literary boastfulness is a more widespread vice. Consider so-called 'hate reading'. Hundreds pore over a column, essay or remark—usually the work of an ideological rival. There is capitalised outrage and snark. The problem is not the frustration or rage itself, which can rightly complement criticism. What ruins hate reading is laziness and often narcissism. It seeks the psychological security of an obvious enemy. And doing so publicly ramps up its braggadocio. As David Hume noted, sympathy can boost the vibrancy and palpability of ideas. With hate reading, the idea of the 'I' itself is augmented: communal fury or mockery leaves attackers with a firmer, more fond grip on themselves. (So to speak.) Columns written to provide this pleasure—'yellow journalism' a century ago, now 'clickbait'—are literally exercises in vanity: for the readers.

But hate readers do not deserve to relish their own acuity or moral rectitude. Conceited reading, for all its froth, is torpid. It uses the written word as an existential prop. Posers attack columns or books for their taken-for-granted failings, and do so precisely because they are conveniently shallow or clumsy—or seem so. Because of this, arrogant audiences squander their liberty. The author's labours are trivialised. And the reader's leisure is spent securing a brittle superiority, which requires ever more sarcasm or hectoring to keep from cracking under reality's weight.

In this, vain reading is a betrayal of the basic literary covenant. The author offers her words at liberty, and the reader freely accepts responsibility for rendering them. This bond can be suspicious, resentful, adoring, respectful or weary. But it asks for a basic commitment from both partners. Vanity abandons this affiliation for a kind of selfishness: the text only exists to paper over the widening seams of the ego. Clerics chase phantoms instead of refining their theology. Commenters devote days to communal harrumph, rather than studying the best of their adversaries' ideas. As with so many privative withdrawals, the hate reader risks a great deal by huffily abandoning good company.

THE HEART HAS ITS REASONS

To overcome vain reading we need humility, which asks for no special protection. Existentially naked, we confront our own imperfections. Yet this too can lapse into a vice.

Take Blaise Pascal, the seventeenth-century French mathematician and philosopher. At first blush, Pascal seems a straightforward opponent of modesty. In correspondence with some of the greatest scholars of his age, including René Descartes and Pierre de Fermat, Pascal was intellectually confident and did not doubt the value of cognitive talent. He pitied fools who thought themselves wise. In his *Pensées*, he asked why someone's lame leg causes no consternation, but an equally crippled mind offends. 'Because a lame man recognises that we are walking straight,' he answered, 'while a lame mind says that it is we who are limping.' To give up on the rigours of reason was, for Pascal, to waste a unique human gift.

Pascal believed that the intellect was divinely given to better comprehend the universe: its laws and facts, including his own pioneering work on probability and the vacuum. 'Man is only a reed, the weakest in nature,' he wrote famously, 'but he

is a thinking reed.' Reflection was also fundamental for revealing the human condition. He argued that daily life is a restless flight from boredom and pain. 'Diversion passes our time,'
he wrote, 'and brings us imperceptibly to our death.' We are
always running away from mortality, said Pascal, and from the
recognition that our annihilation happens all too soon, in a
pointless mechanical universe. Behind the distractions of cash,
fame or lust is an empty, dead cosmos, waiting to envelop us.
'I see only infinity on every side, hemming me in like an atom,'
Pascal confessed, 'or like the shadow of a fleeting instant.'

Yet Pascal was no enlightenment philosophe, deserting
faith for the city of reason. On the contrary, he was a fervent
and eventually austere Christian, devoting most of his later
life, including his *Pensées,* to theological argument. Scientific
research and philosophical analysis allowed Pascal to realise
the truth of cosmic indifference—they were not enough to
cope with it. He needed hope to continue, and faith took
over where reason failed. 'The heart has its reasons,' he wrote,
'of which reason knows nothing.' Ordinary scholarship fails
to calculate the natural universe, Pascal argued, and has no
chance with the supernatural. Intelligence is best when it
knows its limits and has the discipline to think boldly within
them—and no further.

This humility characterised Pascal's reading of scripture.
Like Augustine, Pascal believed that the point was charity: the
Bible ought to leave the reader loving God. And if passages in
the scriptures depart from this, the good Christian 'reconciles
all contradictions'. When *Exodus* promises a messiah bringing
his people to the promised land, for example, these are
metaphors: for Christ offering the Kingdom of God to all.
The 'carnal Jews', said Pascal, read their own scriptures too
literally. It was up to Jesus and Paul to give a key to the code:

'when the word of God, which is true, is false in the letter it is true in spirit'. In other words, the job of scholarship is not to falsify any part of the scriptures, but to demonstrate its eternal verities. The testaments ask for thought, not doubt. Whatever happens, the Bible is *always* right.

Pascal was a man of his era. While he worked alongside libertines and doubters, many of these were simply worldly Christians—they took issue with clerics or biblical command-ments, but not with faith itself. Even Voltaire, who a century later harangued the French church for its cruelties and blun-ders, was a deist. His was a god of reason without a miraculous son, but a god nonetheless. This was a world in which divin-ity was real and good, and there was no prominent conflict between thinking and reverence. For much of the seventeenth century, atheism was more commonly a slur than a worked-out philosophy of godlessness. In this often lax milieu, Pascal took up the ardent Christianity of the Jansenists. Fiercely penitent, the Jansenists believed in a pure Augustinian faith. Mankind is wholly corrupted, they argued, and only God's grace is redemptive: we are free to be evil, not good. To even take communion, a life of severe piety and meekness before the Lord is required. (As in Protestantism, this changes noth-ing in God's plan. It only suggests that certain souls are not damned.) 'Do not be astonished to see simple people believ-ing without argument,' he wrote in *Pensées*. 'God makes them love him and hate themselves. He inclines their hearts to believe.' In this, Pascal was more grave than most of his rich, educated peers, but his relationship to the holy word was not unique—he was part of a community of forceful worship, in an era of faith.

Yes his mind and drive were rare. A child prodigy who became an equally gifted scientist and mathematician, Pascal need not have bowed to the absolute truth of Christian scripture. He was capable of faith, virtue—and scepticism. But Pascal confronted the Bible and said 'yes' to all of it.

MEN DESTROYED

Pascal was a favoured author of Friedrich Nietzsche, who also diagnosed the problem with Pascal's reading. The German philosopher saw Pascal as a fellow critic of superficiality and hypocrisy. When Nietzsche wrote in *Human, All Too Human* that 'haste is universal because everyone is in flight from himself,' he was echoing one of Pascal's hobbyhorses: labour as a pointless escape from reality. He praised Pascal for his willingness to stop and reflect rigorously, instead of busying himself with 'antlike industry'.

Nietzsche also saw the French thinker as an exemplar of religious discipline. The church forced its best souls, like Pascal and Descartes, to be intellectually severe. The result for Nietzsche was a kind of mental gymnastics: the 'supple audacity' of minds trained with asperity. Knowing personally the gifts of religious fervour and classical cramming, Nietzsche the pastor's son respected those who submitted to authority— as long as this cultivated new strengths.

But Nietzsche was aghast at Pascal's meekness with scripture. He saw this humility as the crippling of an otherwise proud mind. 'One should never forgive Christianity,' he wrote in his late notebooks, 'for having destroyed men like Pascal.' For Nietzsche, the religion of Christ did provide new potencies—it was basically a vampire, gnawing away at the pride of great men. It did this by offering a new ideal of humanity: modest, craven, ashamed of instinct and pleasure, flinching from its own achievements. Christianity seduced some of the strongest souls, those most existentially ambitious and most willing to sacrifice happiness. Faith made their moments of weakness or weariness into their best selves. 'It knows how to make the noble instincts poisonous and sick,' said Nietzsche, 'until their force ... turns against itself.'

In Pascal's case, this was encouraged by his terrible health: a lifelong litany of aches, weakness, nausea and other chronic ailments, some perhaps caused by childhood malnutrition. It also arose from loneliness, as the already low Pascal fell into profound melancholy after his father's death and the loss of his sister to Port-Royal Abbey. Pascal always teetered between mundane swagger and exhausted ennui, but illness and solitude heightened his fervour. Later in his life, he was horribly sick and thought the world was equally ill. The calm that eventually came with this was only achieved with the otherworldliness recommended by Augustine: the good Christian is alienated, sickened by himself, 'a sort of death of the soul'. Then he finds God and gives himself up wholly. '[F]or they see to the extent that they die to the world,' wrote Augustine in *On Christian Teaching*, 'and to the extent that they live in it they fail to see.' Pascal's happiness required a rejection of ordinary life and bowed submission to the Lord.

So Pascal, a man of intellectual power and pride, was humbled. Instead of facing 'the terrifying spaces of the universe' and pushing on alone, the French scholar clung to his gospel. His analytic mind tore up every paper-thin shibboleth of worldly vanity, but left the scriptures whole. 'How I hate such foolishness as not believing in the Eucharist, etc,' wrote Pascal. 'If the Gospel is true, if Jesus Christ is God, where is the difficulty?' A fair point for the faithful, but only when that innocuous 'if' is left without scrutiny. Pascal took the truth of the Bible for granted, and his reading was often unquestioning at best. He saw *Exodus*, for example, as a straightforward historical document, and was unusually naïve as he tried to prove the worth of prophecies or the truth of miracles. 'Why can not a virgin produce a child? Does not a hen produce eggs without a cock?' In this, Pascal displayed what scholar Donald Adamson called 'a degree of credulity unbefitting either a natural scientist or a historian'. His more profound problem, for Nietzsche, was his longing for metaphysical compensation; for a guarantee of divine meaning behind the empty infinities of space and time. Proud minds, Nietzsche wrote in 'The Wanderer and His Shadow', do not need this certainty 'any more than the ant needs them to be a good ant'.

The point is not that Christian scripture *must* be false, but that Pascal, a man of immense intelligence, gave up asking the question. And he gave it up, not out of exhaustion or exasperation, but out of humility—Christ's creed had transformed 'proud assurance into unease and qualms of conscience', as Nietzsche put it.

For Nietzsche, Pascal was a victim of his own pusilla-nimity, what Aristotle described as 'unduly retiring'. While the vain man steals others' plaudits, the pusillanimous man avoids success and denies kudos. Aristotle wrote of this overly modest man as 'small-minded'. Interestingly, the Greek philosopher argued that this vice was worse than arrogance. It was 'commoner', he wrote, and suggested a weak interest in great things. Again, this was partly Aristotle's aristocratic contempt for ordinary caution. But it was also a reasonable wariness of citizens who failed to make use of their skills. The faint-hearted were not to be trusted to excel for the greater good.

Over a millennium later, theologian Thomas Aquinas took up Aristotle's portrait of extreme modesty. It was 'contrary to a law of nature', he wrote in his *Summa Theologica*.

Everything, whether animal or plant, strives to make the best use of its power, but the fainthearted shrink from this God-given mission. Aquinas, Aristotle and Nietzsche had conflicting ideas about what this mission was. The theologian's pious ambitions were far removed from those of the Greek aristocrat or German 'Antichrist'. Still, there was a basic consensus on this broken meekness: a failure to realise potential, because of a false idea of lowliness.

Pascal, for all his talent, was reading too faintheartedly. He was a fierce enemy of worldly idols and a precise analyst of physical and mathematical laws. Nietzsche referred to him as one of the 'great moralists', able to distance themselves from common illusions. But when it came to scripture, Pascal lost his characteristic critical eye. He became small, deferential, hobbled by credulity. Pascal overcame vanity, but erred on the side of modesty.

EDITING REVELATION

To read well, pride is necessary. Not arrogance or hubris, but a careful, critical intellect, unhampered by deferential lowliness.

A good example of proud reading comes from Alfred North Whitehead. Like Pascal, Whitehead was a philosopher, mathematician and careful analyst of humanity. Born in the middle of the nineteenth century, he read the scriptures in Greek as a boy, and quoted verses spontaneously in conversation. But where Pascal was conservative, Whitehead was happy to take liberties.

In *Adventures of Ideas*, he suggested that the New Testament needed revising. A better ending, he argued, was Pericles's funeral oration, from fifth-century Athens. Pericles's speech was recorded in Thucydides's *History of the*

Peloponnesian War, which detailed the savage conflict between Athens, Sparta and allied states. Pericles's eulogy was given at the end of the war's first year, and was a tribute to the city itself. Instead of John the Divine's cataclysmic warnings, the speech celebrated tolerance. Pericles called Athens an 'education to Greece', and praised the city for its intellectual and artistic gifts, and atmosphere of liberty. 'We do not get into a state with our next-door neighbour,' he said, 'if he enjoys himself in his own way, nor do we give him … black looks'. No doubt Pericles was idealising Athens, just as Thucydides was editorialising the oration. But the ideal itself is striking: an offering of harmony, instead of divine punishment.

For Whitehead, the Bible fell short of this message by concluding with a barbaric argument of force: 'one will imposing itself on other wills'. God did not reveal beautiful verity or even convince with logic—he threatened with eternal torture ('whosoever was not found written in the book of life was cast into the lake of fire'). Pericles lauded a balance between liberty and unity, art and politics, physical and intellectual effort, and this Athenian model was for emulation not coercion. Whitehead described it as 'action weaving itself into a texture of persuasive beauty'. So whereas Pascal's vision of scripture required submission, Whitehead saw in Thucydides's passages an invitation. The words were an appeal to free Greeks, not a browbeating for unruly pagans.

Whitehead's editorial suggestions might seem arrogant: the meddling of a secular philosopher, looking down on faith. But Whitehead respected religion. He read scripture critically because he believed the religious outlook was vital for civilisation, and the Bible often corrupted this vision.

AS BAD AS DRINK

To understand Whitehead's unorthodox reading, it helps to know a little about his beliefs. While his arguments were sophisticated, this phrase makes a helpful epigraph for Whitehead's philosophy: 'No fact is merely itself'. His point was not that there is no such thing as fact or fiction, true or false. Instead, Whitehead was noting that any one thing is always part of a broader and deeper mess of things. And the word 'things' is misleading. It suggests little islands of matter, floating on a sea of gas or nothingness. But, argued Whitehead, all things are actually processes: reaching out to one another in (and as) time and space. Whitehead's word for the basic stuff of existence was 'activity', and nature is a 'theatre for the inter-relations of activities'. A thing, in this outlook, is not something that simply is—it is something that *happens*: it arises from, and dives back into, a lather of to-and-fro. Most everyday objects are 'societies', made up of processes coming together in this way.

For Whitehead, humans are societies too—but we forget we have risen out of the bubble and spray. Like David Hume, we often focus on what Whitehead called 'clear and distinct sensory experiences': light and colour here, sounds there, touch here. It is literally superficial, concerned with the sensory surface of the world, rather than the frothy depths. These faculties give us a false sense of clarity. The world *seems* divided into neat spatial regions, which never touch one another. This outlook makes sense of time in the same way. Days become a series of ticks and tocks, none of which ever meet. Workaday life has a commonsense simplicity to it: a universe of well-mannered things that keep to themselves.

The problem, for Whitehead, is that this vision of the world is deceptively simple, and slows civilised progress. By treating everything as little atoms, we become doctrinaire. We see human beings as 'things'—at best, just solitary facts; at worst, as tools or commodities to be used or exchanged. Communities are ignored in favour of individuals, the past and future for the present. For all our specialist knowledge, we lose 'that sense of vast alternatives, magnificent or hateful', Whitehead wrote, 'lurking in the background, and awaiting to overwhelm our safe little traditions'. Religion, he argued, is the urge that keeps us in touch with these enormities.

This perception of depth and breadth is vital for reading. Spoken language is itself superficial: easily heard and remembered sounds, which stand out from the hubbub. We use these noises to recall, refine and refute ideas; to signal feelings and note perceptions. But for Whitehead, speech is always in and of a specific time and place; always knotted in the tangle of existence. The words are 'immersed in the immediacy of social intercourse', as he put it. The voice itself is visceral, a reminder of our bodily involvement in activity. Echoing his beloved author Plato, Whitehead argued that the written word is often removed from this rich background.

So Christian scripture, like all writing, is a portable piece of the sensory world. It is at home in specific places and times—but it can travel. It contains splinters of life, which encourage readers to forget they are fragmented. So the book of *Revelation*, which Pascal saw as a timeless verity, is actually what Whitehead called an 'abstraction from insistent surroundings'. It requires a critical sense of history and philosophy to better interpret its truths—and its falsehoods.

How is this achieved? Not simply with some solitary genius. In 'Universities and Their Function', Whitehead praised the 'self-confidence derived from pride in the achievements of the surrounding society'. His point was that civilised doubt and intellectual precision are never gained alone. The proud reader takes pleasure, not in mere cleverness, but in the traditions that support reflection and speculation in the first place—the inheritance we invest every time we read. Readers, like texts, also have histories.

Pascal, in this light, was a man of his era, and deserves to be read as a seventeenth-century iconoclast, not as a failed modern. We need not lambaste him for his errors, but simply try to avoid them. He did not read the Bible with the independence and scepticism he brought to psychology or physics; he flinched as he touched infinities. Pascal provides a dignified warning: not to reify the written word, tugging a forelock to its sacred perfection. For Whitehead, readings like Pascal's actually paralyse religion by narrowing and hardening its view. To best contribute to a civilised life, scripture asks for curious respect, not literal obedience.

So Whitehead's attitude to the Bible was one of pride, not vanity. He read scripture carefully, in more than one language, and was familiar with the ideas of theologians like Augustine, Aquinas and Luther. He was keenly aware of his own small standpoint on the universe, and revered the Bible's 'suggestion of infinitude'; the reminder that there are always more possibilities than we recognise. Whitehead was not claiming revelation beyond his talent or labours. Yet he was not renouncing his own investigative intellect, or capacious imagination. 'Do not get a mere craving for print without thought,' Whitehead told schoolboys in 1919. 'It is almost as bad as drink.'

NO GOD'S-EYE VIEW

Vanity and pusillanimity are not limited to religious dogma or novels. And these vices go beyond commentary and punditry. For every fundamentalist Christian there is a JRR Tolkien fanatic who cannot see the conservative, nostalgic ethos of Middle Earth and its petty bourgeois saviours—what novelist Michael Moorcock called 'Winnie-the-Pooh posing as an epic'. And for every fan, there is a snob who dismisses the intricacies of Tolkien's *The Silmarillion* as schoolboy fantasy, forgetting the scholarship behind it. Likewise for the novels of Emily Brontë or Ernest Hemingway, or the dialogues of Plato—each has its arrogant enemies and too-humble acolytes. Someone's love—of a god, hero, utopia, flattering climax—can invite deference or denial in equal measure.

To cultivate pride, adored works or authors must be met with a mood of query. A little graffiti can help. Author Tim Parks argued that marginalia break the spell of inviolate holiness. 'There is something predatory, cruel even, about a pen suspended over a text,' Parks said. 'Like a hawk over a field, it is on the lookout for something vulnerable. Then it is a pleasure to swoop and skewer the victim with the nib's sharp point.' Parks's metaphor suggests bite and venom, though the endgame is more violation than predation: sullying the pages' aura of spotless sanctity.

More importantly, the proud reader becomes intimate with detractors and defenders, and their roles in a tradition of debate. This is particularly true of classics, which rightly invite reinterpretations and recreations. These are 'the books that come down to us bearing the traces of readings previous to ours', as Italo Calvino put it, 'and bringing in their wake the traces they themselves have left'. A passionate Platonist might study *The Republic* alongside Whitehead's *Modes of Thought* and Martha Nussbaum's *The Fragility of Goodness*. Whitehead defends the philosopher's speculative boldness, while Nussbaum is wary of Plato's longing for certainty and control. A devotee of Kazantzakis might read *The Last Temptation* alongside Simone de Beauvoir's *The Second Sex*, and scrutinise his reduction of women to secondary symbols of sex, death and domesticity. This is what Kazantzakis's meticulous interpreter Peter Bien called 'a blind spot in a vision that, otherwise, is often broad and clear'. In each case, our readings grow out of the mulch of past responses, and become the humus for future replies.

The idea is not to pass down *the* final judgement on Plato, Kazantzakis, Pascal or any other author. There is no such assessment. This debate simply promotes the critic's pride: a willingness to recognise the best in a text, without turning it into a hallowed relic or infallible commandment.

Ironically, this pride arises from an awareness of smallness and transience. For Whitehead, we are tiny parts of a dynamic whole; only brief confluences of energy in an enormous universe. To see literary works as fallible is to recognise our own errors, ambiguities and vicissitudes. We reflect proudly on writings, sacred or profane, precisely because we do not have a God's-eye view; because pronouncements of perfection are always flawed. Pride can be the pleasure we take in thinking ambitiously about our own humble finitude.

TEMPERANCE

Appetite for Distraction

Some nights have the atmosphere of a sigh: a slow release of the chest's day-long tightness. Chores ticked and shoes kicked off, I eased my back into the couch. The schoolboy and preschooler were snoring fitfully. Ruth, my wife, was also asleep—still holding Shirley Hazzard's *The Great Fire*. Sinking into solitude, I grabbed the fiction equivalent of a cold beer: a Star Trek novel. I tapped my tablet and read: 'Will Riker … drifted in freefall, a few meters away from the lab's central observation platform'. I too floated not so boldly into this new world.

But it was not new to me. For almost three decades, I had followed Riker on television, in films and prose. This novel, *The Red King*, portrayed the twenty-fourth-century officer with a new crew and starship. But its universe was comfortably familiar. I relaxed into the story, rolling down its gently sloping plot, mind in neutral. My destination was not sleep, but the next volume in the series, which I looked up as soon as I finished *The Red King*'s last lines. ('Take it away.') The transaction was more tic than choice. Before buying the sequel, I avoided philosophical reflection: on Star Trek's psychology of command, politics of exploration, or aesthetics of xenobiology. This was easeful consumption, compulsively enjoyed.

The Star Trek franchise succeeded where Dan Brown failed, affording preoccupation without interruption. With the help of Will Riker and his liberal pluralist crew, I achieved a relaxed vacuity. Years later, I cannot remember *The Red King*'s plot. After reading the portentous blurb—'his crew struggles with the scientific and philosophical implications of what they discover'—the vacancy still continues. Even the mood is a question mark, which is unusual. Normally the ambiance of a novel remains: the psychodrama of Deborah Levy's magnificent *Swimming Home*, or the leisured idiocy of Wodehouse's Jeeves series. *The Red King* and its sequels left no lingering atmosphere. For all the hours and dollars spent on their prose, these novels made a hole in my memory.

More than a third of the fiction archived on my tablet is from the Star Trek franchise. All purchased over eight months, and most deleted once finished. There was a criminal tidiness to this: cleaning up the scene of the crime. The transgression was not in the genre, but in my reading of it. Buying sequel after sequel, pausing for Earl Grey but not thought, I felt addicted, and this habit was ugly to me.

BELLY GODS

What I found repugnant in myself was called *akolasia* by Aristotle: intemperance, indulgence. It is a poorly managed appetite for food, drink and sex—the senses of touch, rather than sight or hearing. Aristotle's criticism was not of appetites in themselves, but those unguided by reason. To suffer *akolasia* is to have uncontrolled hunger, thirst or lust. He wrote of the 'belly gods' who stuffed themselves at every chance. Others were not gluttons, but had tastes that left them worse off: drunk, sluggish, jittery or just ill. Intemperance is an appetite for the wrong things, or too much of the right things. It is a failure, not of will, but of value. The indulgent person, wrote Aristotle, 'loves such pleasures more than they are worth'.

While the philosopher focused on touch, he recognised that intemperance was often used more broadly. Children, he argued, were often indulgent in general, having trouble pulling back on all their appetites. They had to learn what was healthy, how much to enjoy, and not simply with desserts or sweetened wine. Elaborating Aristotle's points, Thomas Aquinas argued that we use the word 'intemperance' to refer to a more common failure: 'the inclination of animal nature that is not subject to reason'.

This failure, said Aquinas, was 'bestial', and Aristotle used similar language. In his *Republic*, Plato said the indulgent soul resembled a city in which 'children and women and slaves … and base rabble' are free from the commands of the noble minority. Plato's chauvinism is abhorrent, but the impression of ugliness is familiar. Intemperance is a lack of mental order. This adds an aesthetic dimension to the ethical criticism: not merely an appetite for nasty things, but a misshapen psyche.

This is why I grimaced at my Star Trek habit. When I kept clicking 'buy', I was revealing a psychological disorder in the original sense: a lack of proper proportion. A generous critic might diagnose hypochondria, finding an illness in harmless pulp. Certainly, this was not literally an addiction to meals, booze or flesh, and it passed within a year. Nonetheless, it was a badly managed craving for psychological repose. In that moment of leisured exhalation, I gave in. The USS *Titan* returned, along with my rush to spend scarce cash and hours on literally forgettable worlds. It was what Aristotle described as 'slavish character'. I became accustomed to the relief of escapism, and the impression was rightly unflattering.

But there is more to *akolasia* than ugliness. It can also be harmful, because we lose sight of what is worthwhile. Take booze. Aquinas argued that getting plastered deliberately was most sinful, since when a Christian 'willingly and knowingly deprives himself of the use of reason' she also makes other sins more likely. After quaffing: gambling, adultery, assault. These can waste money, break marriages, and sever friendships or civil society. So the loss of rationality hindered 'not only on the requirements of the body, but also on the requirements of external things, such as riches and station, and more still on the requirements of good conduct'. This is a more general point about value: indulgence can corrupt health, tarnish reputations and compromise ethics, because it puts the wrong things first. It is 'disgraceful', to use Aristotle's word, because it sacrifices what we normally esteem.

My Star Trek obsession was a relatively benign example of this. I did not fall into Aquinas's drunken stupor, but I did fail to control myself. I might have read Brian Aldiss or John Brunner, whose novels are as speculative as *Star Trek*— often more so. They also involve critiques of contemporary shibboleths, resisting easy reassurance. I chose the most familiar universe, one with an often complacent view of liberal niceness. And I did so repeatedly, shirking the new and sophisticated in favour of the old and simplistic. I shrank from surprise, challenge, risk, and revelled in a comfortable universe. What was increasingly lost was neither wealth nor status, as Aquinas warned, but regulation of perception. My lucidity flagged.

A LITERARY CENSER

It might seem strange to see dishonesty as a kind of appetite. But the Anglo-Irish philosopher Iris Murdoch believed that it was normal to long for some calming elsewhere. We are, she believed, basically deluded animals. The ego twists and ripples reality to keep itself comfortable—an existential post-production that includes the erasure of its own selfishness. Murdoch's point was not that we must be this way, simply that we usually are. Illusion and egotism are our default. 'Consciousness is not normally a transparent glass through which it views the world,' Murdoch wrote in 'The Sovereignty of Good Over Other Concepts', 'but a cloud of more or less fantastic reverie designed to protect the psyche from pain.'

For Murdoch, ethics is not simply about calculation and choice: giving values to laws or deeds, adding up the pluses and minuses, and coming up with a score. Morality is chiefly about consciousness, a psyche able to perceive without distortion. She was a moral realist, believing that there is a right way to comprehend the cosmos. Influenced by Plato, Murdoch argued that morality asks for a kind of knowledge— not only about facts, but also about the ultimate principles with which we judge these facts. To be immoral is to suffer from a corrupted intimacy with the world, in which the desire for deception is unchecked.

Literature can be vital for this struggle. Murdoch believed that art, at its best, was an invitation to reunite with real-ity. It asks for sensitive and sustained concentration, without restless fancy. Murdoch's theory resembles Dewey's in parts, describing a unity that beckons attention. Next to the piece-meal flux of everyday life, we find a vision of completeness. In this way, art gestures at perfection: a glimpse of goodness. Goodness is not a thing, Murdoch argued, but that by which we judge all things—a principle of ultimate worth. Because of this, the good is worthwhile for its own sake, not for anything other than itself. 'We surrender ourselves to its authority,' she wrote, 'with a love which is unpossessive and unselfish.' Great literature affords a chance to be drawn away from our ego-centric fantasies.

Murdoch's theory was, and still is, out of step with con-temporary English-speaking philosophy. Its Platonism seems otherworldly; its interest in transcendence vague. And certainly it is no easy hypothesis to prove or refute. But Murdoch's point about consciousness is compelling. Ethics requires more than a personal account of good and bad, and the freedom to decide either way. It also asks for a basic willingness to approach the world honestly; to develop a passion for truth, instead of com-forting deception. This more generous view of the world is what Murdoch called 'unselfing'.

In Murdoch's language, my Star Trek binge was selfing: taking my all-too-human holiday from reality, and extending my visa. While Murdoch used the trope of sight instead of touch, she had in common with Plato, Aristotle and Aquinas a wariness of unguided appetite. My binge was not a collapse of will, but a mistaken attachment to numbing semblance. If consciousness is, as Murdoch suggested, a cloud of daydreams, then I used *The Red King* and its sequels as a literary censer.

THE MOST DANGEROUS MAN

My turn away from fantasy was encouraged by philosophy. To begin, my discipline is cautious of desire. This goes back at least to Plato's wariness of 'bestial' gratification. It is part of a long tradition of suspicion, which German philosopher Peter Sloterdijk called 'loser romanticism'. Scholarship need not carve off body from mind, lust from cognition, but it helps to be careful of appetite—if only so it can be well deployed. This is an ancient Platonic maxim: it matters what we love.

Philosophy also provided specific books to remedy my malaise. One of my next purchases after the final Star Trek was *Language, Truth and Logic* by English philosopher AJ Ayer. Finished when the author was only twenty-five and still a student at Oxford, this treatise was a bold and damaging attack on mainstream philosophy in the early twentieth century.

The power of Ayer's book to undo my selfishness came from its prose style, but also its philosophical radicalism. This school of thought, known chiefly as logical positivism, rejected many of the long-held ideas of Western scholarship. Ayer was once described as 'the most dangerous man' in Oxford for his wholesale rubbishing of much of the canon. He argued that philosophy's job is not to provide fundamental concepts of existence: so-called 'first principles', with which all truths can be discovered. The philosopher does not reveal esoteric reality or draw up moral legislation. Philosophy simply analyses the kinds of statements we can make. Take the sentence 'Ayer once argued with heavyweight boxer Mike Tyson at a party'. It might be weird, but it simply asks for proof. (Yes, the spat happened. The most dangerous man at Oxford prevailed.) The sentence 'Ayer once danced with the intangible spirit of

Captain William Riker' makes no sense. Not because it con-
tradicts English grammar, but because it cannot be reason-
ably accepted or rejected either way. By definition, the event
is beyond physical proof, and so it is 'literally nonsensical', in
Ayer's words. There are propositions that ask for no evidence,
like those of logic and mathematics, but they tell us nothing
new: they are all tautologies, said Ayer. They reveal the rules
of language and reason, without which nothing can be said
and thought.

Philosophy, in Ayer's sense, is a referee in the game of
knowledge. It does not play, so much as judge the play of
others. Is your statement testable with experience, or rationally necessary? If not, get off the field.

This was a shock to many scholars. From Plato's Forms
to Heidegger's Being, philosophy was a history of mistakes
with language. Perhaps more worrying to many, Ayer's outlook made ethics look dubious. He argued that morality is
chiefly about preferences: neither facts nor logic, but rather
statements of approval or disapproval. 'They are pure expres-
sions of feeling,' Ayer wrote, 'and as such do not come under
the category of truth and falsehood.' Moral statements
might prompt shock or flight, but they afford no moral facts.
Genuine ethical philosophy is, for Ayer, just more policing of
language: defining the terms.

This might seem a meandering reply to literary intemperance. AJ Ayer's philosopher umpire is a world away from
Murdoch's philosophical seer. Indeed, Ayer's outlook is exactly
what Murdoch was responding to. It was his brand of modern
egocentrism that she hoped to overcome: the idea that morality is nothing more than a thin sheet of individual values,
thrown casually over the world. Ayer saw philosophy as a
neutral judge of conversations, whereas Murdoch believed

that ethicists had to take a stance. 'How can we make ourselves better?' Murdoch wrote, 'is a question moral philosophers should attempt to answer.' In ideas, prose style, manner
and temperament, Murdoch and Ayer were inhabiting distant poles.

Yet it was Ayer who helped to turn my gaze back to
the world; who loosened my grip on Star Trek's fantasy. His
phrasing, with its curt immediacy, holds a challenge. It is
combative not consoling. Take Ayer's first line: 'The traditional
disputes of philosophers are, for the most part, as unwarranted
as they are unfruitful'. This is a common sentiment among
philosophers, including Ayer's own scholarly ancestor David
Hume: behold the arrival of a brave truth-bringer. But the
young Oxford student put it with gusto, and a pleasing
cadence. Note the twinned 'un' prefixes and the clause that
helps to draw out the conclusion's coup. Not all of *Language,
Truth and Logic* is this punchy, but as a work of philosophy it
is a lungful of clean air after weeks of incense.

This phrasing held my focus like a science fiction novel,
but Ayer refused any comforts. This was not chiefly a matter
of argument, but of mood. Ayer coaxed me away from covetous reverie, towards public facts and the language to recognise them. It was ontologically miserly, refusing all kinds of
existence. While speculative philosophers rightly take issue
with this approach, the consequences for my consciousness
were immediate. I met with resistance: not dramatic tension
to be easily resolved, but the psychological force that pulled
me away from fancy. I *could* have interpreted Ayer's words
arbitrarily, or with whimsy, but it would have been nonsense—
a waste of his labours and mine. The only way to make sense
of *Language, Truth and Logic* was to take it seriously as a portrait of reality; and, in doing so, overcome my own solipsism.

Comprehension required passion for a foreign cosmos and fidelity to its specificity.

Murdoch herself described this transformation in 'The Sovereignty of Good Over Other Concepts'. Alongside the fine arts, she also discussed education in crafts, mathematics and language. With these pursuits, I cannot be overly inward. I meet a world that shoves me back and refuses to be reduced to my imaginary universe. 'My work is a progressive revelation of something which exists independently of me,' she wrote, 'something which my consciousness cannot take over, swallow up, deny or make unreal.' Murdoch did not recommend Ayer for this task, describing his debut elsewhere as 'brilliant and ingenious, but also unsophisticated and dotty'. But her description of the movement from delusion to truth echoes my remedial reading of Ayer. This is literature that invited recognition of, and respect for, principles outside my own psyche. *Language, Truth and Logic* helped to lessen my intemperance, by providing an object that objected: to my state of mind.

WHY AREN'T THEY SCREAMING?

Ayer is not the only invitation to temperance. For some readers his bravado might be the perfect indulgence: a refusal of messiness, as the whole of scholarship is tidied up into facts and tautologies. In her *Metaphysics as a Guide to Morals*, Murdoch wrote that Ayer's debut 'diminishes the human scene to the state of a logical puzzle', and some do prefer puzzles to the dilemmas of mortality. What looks like academic sobriety can be a gentle literary drug—the mead of abstraction. Ayer was just right for me, but others might seek psychological balance in fiction, essays or poetry.

Virginia Woolf has an idiosyncratic but compelling vision of the world; a refusal to look away from madness, pettiness, alienation. The passages on shell-shocked veteran Septimus, in her novel *Mrs Dalloway*, afford a lingering portrait of a man alone with his insanity:

> A sparrow perched on the railing opposite chirped Septimus, Septimus, four or five times over and went on, drawing its notes out, to sing freshly and piercingly in Greek words how there is no crime and, joined by another sparrow, they sang in voices prolonged and piercing in Greek words, from trees in the meadow of life beyond a river where the dead walk, how there is no death.
>
> There was his hand; there the dead. White things were assembling behind the railings opposite. But he dared not look.

There is pity and patience in Woolf's view, but also bravery: she will not relent. Likewise for her essays like 'The Death of the Moth'. They are elegant in imagery and rhythmic in composition, but will not gratify an appetite for comfort.

Philip Larkin's poetry provides a steady bleakness of gaze. His poem 'The Old Fools' portrays the indignity of age. He writes of mouths gaping, running with spit, and urine dribbling. We stand at the foot of 'extinction's alp', the earth rising up beneath us to meet the end. Larkin's chilling question 'Why aren't they screaming?' speaks to a haunted chase for life, but also at the impossibility of winning this race. It all ends the same way, and the poet's refusal to romanticise mortality is painful but honest. He asks if the elderly know this, and why they are not protesting. His final line includes us all in the contemptible decay: 'Well, / We shall find out.'

Closer to Star Trek in scenes if not themes, Brian Aldiss's *The Dark Light Years* is a confrontation with the alien strangeness of human psychology and society. What seems like an absurd premise—a civilisation that worships shit— is a profound meditation on disgust, fear and sacrament. Aldiss's English is crisp, his characters subtle and his plotting careful. Together with the high weirdness of his world, Aldiss's story attracts, holds, then reorients attention: towards discomfiting humanity.

My particular literary indulgence is not the only kind. Some have unchecked urges for gore, climax or archaic sorcery. There are military esoterica boffins and Dumas devotees. I once binged on Dostoyevsky for the buzz of his sweaty, paling protagonists. What unites these readers is a failure of desire: craving misguidedly or without restraint. The consequence is not, as in Aristotle's conception, obesity, weakness, unpopularity or poverty; not loss of health or station. What suffers with intemperance is consciousness: like Catherine Morland in Austen's *Northanger Abbey*, pages are used to avoid what is pressing or precious; to feed delusion instead of starving it. The problem is not the novel, which demonstrates what Austen called a 'most thorough knowledge of human nature, the happiest delineation of its varieties', along with humour and craftsmanship. The problem is Catherine's indulgence in Gothic fantasy, haunted by her warped sense of worth.

Literary *akolasia* is a failure to see clearly, and this changes from mind to mind, day to day. Some days I need a little Captain Riker to compensate for my harassed pessimism.

ANOREXIA

Rarer than intemperance is literary *anorexia*: literally lack
of appetite, in Ancient Greek. Aristotle barely discussed
this, because 'such insensibility', in his words, 'is not human'.
The philosopher was not arguing that we never refuse grub
or booze; that it is utterly alien to avoid a bedtime quickie
in favour of a paperback. Aristotle was rightly noting that
everyone hungers and thirsts, and most lust—it is an organic
response to animal existence. We might have varied tastes or
a cycling libido, but we will still long for *something*. 'If there
is any one who finds nothing pleasant and nothing more
attractive than anything else,' wrote Aristotle, 'he must be
something quite different from a man.'

Aristotle's pronouncement asks for caution. Depression
can lead to a general lack of desire. 'I saw that for a long time,'
wrote F Scott Fitzgerald in 'The Crack-Up', 'I had not liked
people and things, but only followed the rickety old pretence
of liking.' In the thirteenth century, Thomas Aquinas also
wrote about *acedia*, or sloth: 'an oppressive sorrow, which …
so weighs upon man's mind, that he wants to do nothing;
thus acid things are also cold'. Perhaps because of monas-
ticism's battles with the 'noontide demon', ennui, Christian
theologians were more sensitive than the pagan Greeks to
this numbness to life. They believed that sloth might first
turn monks away from meals or company, and then eventually from divinity itself.

But Aristotle's general point is clear. It is indulgence
and not *anorexia* that requires caution, because it is the more
common vice. This is also true of literature. Among readers,
it is easier to find binging than cool abstinence, much less
full *anorexia*.

Still, there are occasionally naysayers and contrarians who recommend a withdrawal from the written word. Not because of overweening pride or cowardice, but because of literary surfeit: any more phrases would do harm.

Nineteenth-century German philosopher Arthur Schopenhauer was suspicious of reading. Not because he was a philistine. Quite the contrary, he believed that literary works were 'the quintessence of a mind': a psyche, distilled. A highly cultivated author in his own right, Schopenhauer was passionate about good writing. From his aphorisms in 'On Books and Reading':

> There is nothing that so greatly recreates the mind as the works of the old classic writers. Directly one has been taken up, even if it is only for half-an-hour, one feels as quickly refreshed, relieved, purified, elevated, and strengthened as if one had refreshed oneself at a mountain stream.

Schopenhauer argued that the best books deserved two readings. The second allowed for finer, more reflective interpretations, as the beginning was read in light of the end and the whole work in a new mood.

In this spirit, Schopenhauer also warned against terrible literature. We are mortals, he argued, and there are only so many days left: why squander hours? The philosopher detailed the symptoms of literary disease, and he cautioned his readers against this 'intellectual poison', which sickens the mind. Literary and scientific history, for example, was full of facts but empty of thought. Historians are proud of their magpie hoards, he argued, but these caches of names and dates add nothing to our comprehension of the world.

For the true scholar, this assemblage of stuff is ultimately dissatisfying. 'It is like reading a cookery-book,' wrote Schopenhauer, quoting the scientist and satirist Lichtenberg, 'when you are hungry.'

FOSSILS AND WEEDS

Yet Schopenhauer was also chary of reading in general. In 'On Thinking For Oneself', he argued that thinking and reading are often contrary. Thinking is free and spontaneous—the work of an intellectual vanguard. Reading is usually slavish and plodding; for weak souls, too dependent to reflect for themselves. Great philosophers will scan pages, and earnestly so—they have 'vast' insight, which is always expanding. But most readers lack this strength. 'The thought we read is related to the thought which springs up in ourselves,' he wrote, 'as the fossil-impress of some prehistoric plant to a plant as it buds forth in spring-time.' And for Schopenhauer, treatises and essays were more than just dead impressions. He also treated written works like noxious weeds, which invade our mental landscape. To really cultivate our minds, we have to resist exotic thoughts and allow our own native ideas to develop. The result is increased liberty: a crafting of the self, instead of being shaped by 'alien' others.

Importantly, Schopenhauer was not arguing for a few semesters in the school of life. He was against the common idea, still popular, that simply living is enough to gain wisdom—as if merely bumping up against the world proffers insight. 'Pure empiricism is related to thinking,' he said, 'as eating is to digestion.' Experience has to be transformed by thought, not simply carried about like cud. We must labour at thought.

For Schopenhauer, reading is too often a distraction from this effort. He argued that we are only thinking apes in the weakest sense of the word. Most of our cognitive power is dedicated to survival, serving our craving for the creaturely fundamentals. We are born, we race to fill bellies and empty glands, then we die. We rarely stop to question the point of this existence—we simply try to endure it. 'Man is a poor animal like the rest,' he explained, 'and his powers are meant only to maintain him.' Trying to really comprehend this situation is painful, Schopenhauer argued, which is why we so often turn to texts. They do not encourage revelation about the human condition, they simply afford a diversion from it. 'The safest way of having no thoughts of one's own,' he argued, 'is to take up a book every moment one has nothing else to do.'

It is important to scratch Schopenhauer's rhetorical enamel with a little biographical fact. As a child, student and scholar, he was a regular reader. Despite his warnings, the philosopher's own shelves contained nearly two hundred volumes on science alone (he studied medicine in Göttingen). The local libraries were part of his calculations when choosing to settle in Mannheim or Frankfurt. Biographer Rüdiger Safranski reported that Schopenhauer's unvarying daily routine usually ended up with solitude and printed paper: 'He spent his evenings at home, reading'. Whatever his published attitude to literature, his private pursuits remained predictably bookish.

The subsequent picture is less straightforward, but still intriguing. Schopenhauer esteemed great writings, and presumably classed himself as one of the sovereign thinkers: independent minds, with unique style. He was erudite, devoted to artistry, and disdainful of hacks. But he also saw reading as a threat to emancipation; a surrender to besieging concepts and urges. Thinking is a limb, but reading can be 'a false tooth, a waxen nose'. The impression Schopenhauer gives is that a flagging appetite for the written word can be healthy. By avoiding books, at least for a spell, we can regain our cerebral liberty, and confront the pointless agony that is life.

Interestingly, Schopenhauer's philosophy of escape stressed the absence of desire altogether. In *The World as Will and Idea*, he argued that we must develop a kind of intellectual perception, which comprehends but does not want to possess the world as it is. Owing a great deal to Immanuel Kant but also to Plato, Schopenhauer believed that the true philosopher gives up on ordinary human wants, and instead contemplates the universe with Vedic equanimity. The will negates itself, leading to a liberating nothingness. The sage loses her compulsive urge for reading—and, eventually, for everything else.

This is a long way from Aristotle's *anorexia*, but one aspect remains: the absence of desire. And more importantly, Schopenhauer saw this as a virtue, not a vice. It is healthy, he suggested, to have no appetite for reading, as long as this arises from a more profound longing: to comprehend the world and partially overcome it. At the very least, reading for most of us is a threat to intellectual independence. We, who cannot go 'straight to the book of Nature' like geniuses and true thinkers, read at out peril.

THE LEADEN CEILING

Friedrich Nietzsche, once an avid student of Schopenhauer, came to similar conclusions. Like his fellow German philosopher, he was ambivalent about the written word. He praised great literature (including his own). He was a gifted and well-read scholar, as comfortable with Athenian drama as with German poetry and French philosophy. He recognised the worth of early cramming, conditioning the mind for suppleness and strength. A man without a good schooling, he wrote in his notebooks, 'walks through life without having learned to walk ... his flabby muscles reveal themselves with every step'. For Nietzsche, reading was like any craft. It asked for discipline and regular exercise, to develop reliable habits. In *Human, All Too Human*, he praised his discipline, philology, for promoting interpretive care: delicate, slow, responsive reading. And his autobiography, *Ecce Homo*, contained a portrait of the ideal reader, 'a monster of courage and curiosity ... supple, cunning, cautious, a born adventurer and discoverer'. Nietzsche rightly saw that the written word asked for virtues, even if he emptied these of their moral significance.

But Nietzsche also took the mickey out of scholars, paralysed by decades of textual study. He argued that those who think chiefly with books, barely think at all. There is a clumsy, plodding, musty and airless atmosphere to literary ideas; a nasty mélange of conservatism and automatism. 'Every craft, even if it should have a golden floor,' he wrote, 'has a leaden ceiling over it that presses and presses down upon the soul until that becomes queer and crooked.' He also maintained, in 'Schopenhauer as Educator', that scholars often turn to books from boredom, not curiosity. Instead of amusing themselves, they seek stimulation: the brief high of goading contradiction or flattering agreement.

Nietzsche maintained that long walks and mountain air were more inspiring than hours poring over syllogisms. This was partly physiological. One of the reasons for his academic retirement from Basel in Switzerland was illness:

nausea, headaches and agonising eyestrain. He was literally pained by reading, writing in *Ecce Homo* that 'my eyes alone put an end to all bookwormishness'. But, consistent with his general philosophy, Nietzsche saw his frailty as a gift: a push towards the mastery of his own ideas. He thought and wrote in opposition to his nineteenth-century peers, and saw their written works as stifled and stifling. Intellectual biographer RJ Hollingdale described Nietzsche's later works as 'a species of talking to oneself', and this makes sense of the philosopher's literary solitude. He was often alone, and his response to books echoed this asylum. Texts were company he wanted to refuse. 'We read rarely,' he wrote in *The Gay Science*, 'but not worse on that account.'

As with Schopenhauer, caution is vital here—Nietzsche's use of 'rarely' was deceptive. He often travelled with his own library, frequented bookshops and borrowed from friends. Before moving to a new part of Europe, he checked the local library. Nietzsche scholar Thomas Brobjer estimated that, in the final four years of his sanity, the philosopher purchased a hundred books—about one a fortnight. As Schopenhauer pointed out, merely collecting tomes is not comprehending them. But Nietzsche annotated many of these ('yes', 'no', 'bravo'), and referred to more in his notes. During the years 1887–88, he read philosophers including Baruch Spinoza, Kant and John Stuart Mill (whom he called a 'flathead'), fiction or poetry by Dostoyevsky, Stendhal, Baudelaire, and Tolstoy on religion. Brobjer wrote that Nietzsche's 'reading was of immense value for him … he sacrificed much for the sake of reading.' The romantic legend of the lone alpine iconoclast needs correction.

Nonetheless, if Nietzsche read studiously, he also tried to quarantine his ideas from books on 8-hour walks, during lakeside reveries. Like Schopenhauer, he believed that reading was often a threat to honesty and originality. While he saw his predecessor's contemplative withdrawal as defeated pessimism, he shared Schopenhauer's antipathy towards books; a wish to overcome craving for pages and keep his own conscience. He caricatured talented academics, emptied out by scholasticism: 'mere matches that have to be struck if they are to ignite'. If Nietzsche failed to live up to his own incendiary ideal, the ideal itself still invites the question: might it be healthy to have no appetite for reading? If *akolasia* is a vice, what of *anorexia*?

ON WALKING AWAY

Schopenhauer and Nietzsche were neither sages nor hypocrites, to be given automatic credence or condemnation. It helps to heed their published works and take seriously their warnings. Yet their private habits are equally demonstrative. They reveal what the philosophers valued, rather than what they believed—or wanted audiences to believe. Both devoted themselves to the written word, and read with fervour. But both were also wary of second-hand or lazy interpretations, and the lack of spontaneity in thoughts prompted only by others' phrases. And both complemented their study with other pursuits. Schopenhauer chiefly read in the evenings, after a day of writing, flute playing and poodle walking. (He reportedly made the breed fashionable in Frankfurt.) Alongside books and letters, Nietzsche also enjoyed forests, lakes, dance, opera and—just before his final illness—Italian coffee and ice cream.

To make sense of their ideas and lives, the gastronomic analogy is suggestive. Literary *anorexia* is a lack of appetite, but not because characters are distasteful or arguments unpalatable; not because we are ill and find the consumption of words off-putting. It happens because we are somehow full: of books, pamphlets, magazines or social media snippets. Nikos Kazantzakis once referred to himself as a 'nanny goat', who was hungry but fed himself paper and ink. *Anorexia* arises before a surfeit of pages: when we goats have eaten enough.

As Schopenhauer and Nietzsche's examples suggest, this turn from reading need not be because of tiredness: head on the pillow, phrases blurring and doubling up. In fact, reading while weary can be oddly rewarding. My current bedside tome is *Ardor*, by the great Italian scholar and publisher Roberto Calasso. A typically close study of Vedic myth and philosophy, given in rhythmic prose, *Ardor* can be opaque—at least on the first parsing. But I recognise my confusion and do not blame Calasso for my torpor. His work prompts a mood of metaphysical reverie, which relaxes and primes for dreaming. Comprehension comes later. In this sense, exhaustion can— and sometimes ought to—end serious scholarship, but it does not have to stop interest.

Anorexia can actually arise at moments of sharpest concentration, when perception is acute and intellect keen. It is the feeling that, whatever we are reading, it can now offer nothing more. Take my morning with Schopenhauer and Nietzsche. I begin with the former's abuse of wealthy idlers, who fill free hours with superficial reading: they are 'beasts of the field', he spat in 'On Books and Reading', from *Parerga and Paralipomena*. Schopenhauer attacks the deadening consequences of thinking with others' thoughts, and the corruption of authorial profiteering. He argues that we ought to take recommendations from educated readers not experts, and describes literary history as the 'catalogue of a museum of deformities'. The overall atmosphere is iconoclastic snark, in which laughter mingles with hesitance. I smile at Schopenhauer's quips, while squinting at his curmudgeonly pose of superiority. He ends on the suffering of the best authors, 'tormented to death' by a cruel and stupid public. In short: author as victim.

From this portrait of noble martyrdom I move to Schopenhauer's philosophical son: Nietzsche in *Ecce Homo*. Again the posture of distance, pushing away a vulgar and painful mob. Nietzsche is explaining his own greatness as a kind of taste: not only saying 'no' to mass culture, but also making sure he does not *need* to say 'no'. 'One can merely through the constant need to ward off,' he writes, 'become too weak any longer to defend oneself.' Nietzsche's example is telling: books. He argues that it is 'vicious' to waste the morning's vitality on reading—yet another case of potency squandered in response to others' stimulations. Like Schopenhauer, Nietzsche is criticising his era, and recommending artful solitude. But the younger philosopher is more visceral, like an animal protecting itself. More hedgehog than genius. If Nietzsche thinks himself above others—and he does—it is not his higher morality, but his selfishness that raises him up. He is strong enough to admit his weaknesses, and deftly compensate for them. These autobiographical passages prompt not smugness or pity but verve; the awareness of my own energy built up and pressing for release; a concern for health instead of correct information.

I end *Ecce Homo* with effervescence, but with no interest in reading further. The words are witty, provocative and perspicacious—this is no slur on Schopenhauer or Nietzsche. Still, for now I have read enough. This is partly because of Nietzsche's message of precarious metabolism, which encourages movement not sedentary scanning. I am suddenly aware of my body—what Nietzsche described as a 'great intelligence' in *Thus Spoke Zarathustra*. The philosopher strolled in orchards and stood beneath his *Gedankenbaum*, his 'thought tree'. I will strain at chin-ups in the courtyard, beside a fence of plaited ivy and spider webs. But my closed paperback is more than a gesture of Nietzschean physicality. Informed by his philosophy, I have also reached a point of awareness. I realise that what guides *anorexia* is less a conscious calculation and more a feel for literary nutrition. Nietzsche's judgement helps me to better comprehend Nietzsche's judgement. Having read *Ecce Homo* after Schopenhauer's *Parerga and Paralipomena*, I feel full with ideas and impressions, and these demand digestion, not more consumption.

Anorexia is not a virtue, but part of another: temperance. It is the loss of interest that marks a more profound commitment. Because I want to understand these thinkers as readers, I must stop reading them. Parsing these passages for the tenth time might keep me busy, but it will not add to this argument. Extra hours of study will sabotage my scholarship. Instead of refining these necessary concepts, I will only collect others: Schopenhauer on Plato or physiognomy, Nietzsche on his mother or Wagner. As with Star Trek, I will take comfort in familiarity: facts and phrases, perhaps the snorts that welcome sardonic stylists. By continuing, I will be distracting myself from thinking; and from transforming thinking into this very prose. Better to stack the volumes and walk away.

JUSTICE

No I Said No I Won't No

Virginia Woolf was fed up, and a little disgusted. Was it because of Lytton Strachey, asking her sister if the stain on her white dress was semen? No, that happened over a decade earlier, when sexual banter was still avant-garde—and Woolf had laughed. ('A flood of the sacred fluid seemed to overwhelm us,' she later wrote.) Was it the thought of clothes shopping with a *Vogue* editor? No, that was yet to come, and prompted more fear than boredom or revulsion. 'I tremble & shiver all over,' she said of the planned retail trip, 'at the appalling magnitude of the task'. In August 1922, Woolf's irritation was typically bookish: she was 200 pages into James Joyce's *Ulysses*.

Two years earlier, in 'Modern Fiction', she had cautiously praised the little-known Irish author for his 'spiritual' writing. Joyce refused to provide an obvious and objective world, revealing flux and haziness instead. Woolf was encouraged by this, but she also lamented Joyce's pettiness and vulgarity—she liked his impressionism, but not his impressions. Now, Woolf's wariness had become hostility. The novel began well, she noted in her diary, but soon it was like watching 'a queasy undergraduate scratching his pimples'. Later that month she declared *Ulysses* irrelevant, and was grateful she was not obliged to write about it. It was too obscure. By September, Woolf had finished the novel, declaring it 'illiterate'. It was an undignified, pretentious work of infantile showing off. It had promise, but this was undermined by Joyce's 'callow board school boy' outlook. Writing to her friend, artist and critic Roger Fry, Woolf described *Ulysses* as a painful burden. While she was relishing Marcel Proust's *In Search of Lost Time*, Joyce's work was a duty. She was tied to it 'like a martyr to a stake'. Woolf was not simply left bored or antsy by Joyce—her response was visceral.

INSIDIOUS ENEMIES

In 'How Should One Read a Book?', Woolf wrote of this righteous fury, the reader's contempt for profligate works. 'Are they not criminals, books that have wasted our time and sympathy,' Woolf asked, 'are they not the most insidious enemies of society, corrupters, defilers, the writers of false books, faked books, books that fill the air with decay and disease?'

Woolf was not recommending mockery or whining. She believed that literature deserves exacting scrutiny: judgement of the work as a whole, which examines it beside the very best, like Jane Austen's *Emma* or Daniel Defoe's *Robinson Crusoe*. Masterpieces are complete and 'no cloud of suggestions hangs about them,' she wrote in 'Hours in a Library', 'teasing us with a multitude of irrelevant ideas'. These visions of sufficiency provide literary standards, against which works can be appraised. This, in turn, breathes life into the art itself. Speaking as a novelist as well as a bibliophile, Woolf believed that readers emit their opinions into the atmosphere of words, which are then inhaled by authors. The writers may not see this breath, but it is inside them—it 'tells upon them', she wrote, 'even if it never finds its way into print'. So readers have a critical duty: to the world of letters, alongside themselves.

But Woolf's insults of Joyce were cruel. She did not simply analyse his language or logic, she denigrated his character and class. In 'Mr Bennett and Mrs Brown', Woolf described *Ulysses* as 'the conscious and calculated indecency of a desperate man'. Her diary was more pointed, trivialising the author as a prole-tarian autodidact. 'We all know how distressing they are,' she continued, 'how egotistic, insistent, raw, striking, & ultimately nauseating.' For Woolf, Joyce was a stunted artist, lacking the breeding and cultivation of the genteel classes. Broken weak-lings like TS Eliot coveted this primal potency, she suggested, but not 'normal' bourgeoisie like Virginia Woolf.

It is easy to accuse Woolf of blatant class snobbery, but her position warrants a little subtlety. In many of her essays and talks, Woolf identified with what she called 'the common reader', without the privilege of schooling, let alone university training. Biographer James King described her and her sisters' education as 'leftovers, bits of learning bestowed on them by their father and brothers'. In 'The Leaning Tower', Woolf included herself among the outsiders who will have to trespass on the old estate of the well-to-do, perhaps squashing turf as they do. There is a democratic timbre to Woolf's rhetoric, speaking of 'we' who will now decide what is taught, thought and read—instead of a few rich boys. When critic Desmond MacCarthy suggested this was bad faith, rightfully pointing out her family's wealth and status, Woolf replied angrily. 'No, no, no, my dear Desmond—I really must protest,' she wrote to him privately. 'I never sat on top of a tower! Compare my wretched little 150 pound education with yours.' Writing as a middle-class woman, whose male friends—including her husband, Leonard—were all educated at Oxford or Cambridge, Woolf felt some kinship with the working-class men she lectured to.

But MacCarthy's flechettes, however tainted with sexism and condescension, did not miss their mark. Next to her peers, Woolf lacked education and public standing. Next to most of England, she was part of the elite. The novelist was born into the Victorian upper-middle classes. 'In their current account ... there was always a balance of hundreds of pounds,' wrote Leonard Woolf in *Beginning Again*, 'and both the heavens and justice would have fallen before that balance fell below zero.' Her father was noted nineteenth-century critic Leslie Stephen. The family library, which began Woolf's literary adventures as a teenager, was well stocked and open—among the shelves, she became 'addicted, escapist and ambitious', as biographer Hermione Lee put it. This was a world apart from the childhood of working-class contemporaries like DH Lawrence, whose father was a violent, drunk miner. While exiled from male privilege, Virginia Woolf enjoyed the rewards of capital: economic, social and cultural. She was someone the proletariat were employed by, not with.

When she described *Ulysses* as an 'underbred' book, Woolf's class was showing. For her, the Irish novelist was not as dull as maids ('Talking to the servants from 8 to 1.15 ... is so boring …') or stupid as Joyce's fellow proletarians ('Do you think all the lower classes are naturally idiotic?'). But his origins seemed to get up Woolf's nose, as if she were recoiling from the stink of commoners—witness her talk of raw flesh, pus and nausea. Even without these connotations, Woolf's response to Joyce was patrician. She treated him as she herself was treated by so many Victorian men: as a pitiful creature, full of talent but lacking discipline. As 'one of those undelivered geniuses', Joyce required a long midwifery of analysis and guesswork—a labour she was not willing to suffer.

VIRTUE SCAMPED

To Woolf's credit, she knew she was biased. In her diary, the author admitted she was neither careful nor charitable with *Ulysses*. She only read it once, and it was an 'obscure' novel she did not comprehend. She did not revise her judgement, chiefly because she was not immediately blown away— Joyce sprayed haphazardly with bullets, she wrote, whereas Tolstoy was a blast to the face. Still, Woolf recognised that her conclusion was not decisive or final. She read a considered review of *Ulysses* in *American Nation*, gaining a firmer grasp of the work's significance. Tellingly, after reading the notice she wrote in her diary that she was wilfully against Joyce. Despite TS Eliot's praise (or perhaps because of it), 'I had my back up on purpose'.

This is exactly what Woolf said *not* to do. Her 'How Should One Read a Book?' recommended generosity: giving oneself to the work, without being aloof or guarded. The reader, she argued, is the writer's comrade and collaborator. Before the task of criticism begins, the two must work together to create a universe from language. 'If you hang back, and reserve and criticise at first,' Woolf argued, 'you are preventing yourself from getting the fullest possible value from what you read.' This requires focus and sympathy: a readiness to become the author, insofar as one can. What Woolf's candour reveals is her unwillingness or inability to become Joyce in this way. This was partly because of her class snobbery, but also because of her anxiety. As a 'spiritual' novelist, Joyce was a competitor. Just as Woolf mocked her rival Katherine Mansfield to numb the sting of jealousy, she held the Irishman at arm's length and refused to get closer.

This does not imply that *Ulysses* was a perfect artwork, or that Woolf had to bow to Joyce's bravado. Speaking only for myself, *Mrs Dalloway* is the more moving work; the more nuanced, searching portrait of human fragility and intimacy (or lack of this). Woolf's failure was critical: she did not give herself the chance to enjoy or even recognise Joyce's achievements. She hung back. For all her erudition, sagacity and perception, Virginia Woolf sold *Ulysses* short. 'No doubt,' she wrote in her diary, 'I have scamped the virtue of it more than is fair.'

LED BY SLIGHT INDICATIONS

By mocking his novel without reading it carefully, Woolf did Joyce an injustice. This may seem overly formal or legalistic— as if the Grub Street constabulary might charge Woolf with criminal hatchery. But justice was an ethical impulse before it was law. As Alasdair MacIntyre points out, justice varies with traditions: from Homer to Plato, Aristotle to Augustine. And not only justice, but also the logic with which we comprehend it, and the values that prop it up. Think of the fierce aesthetic conflicts between Edwardian and Georgian writers divided by only a generation, like HG Wells and Woolf herself. Centuries and thousands of miles can profoundly change our sense of righteousness.

But at its most basic, justice is the willingness and ability to give others their dues. In this, it is a distinctly social virtue, which concerns others more than oneself. 'It is not possible,' wrote Aristotle, 'to treat oneself unjustly'.

Aristotle's point was not that we never underestimate or undervalue ourselves. His account of pusillanimity is clear: sometimes we fail to laud our own talents or accomplishments. Witness Virginia Woolf's aching doubt about her own novels, barely assuaged by her husband's praise. ('I must carry the proofs, like a dead cat, to Leonard,' she wrote of *The Years*, '& tell him to burn them unread.') This was a vice for Aristotle, but not injustice, strictly speaking. Justice concerns our treatment of others, and our own mental disharmonies are only unjust metaphorically.

Aristotle noted that we can thieve honour alongside trinkets; that we can wound status alongside flesh. But it is Aquinas who brings out the literary aspects of justice—what he called 'a habit whereby a man renders to each one his due by a constant and perpetual will'. In the *Summa Theologica*, he included injuries to reputation as well as the body. The worst sin was to publicly condemn someone with flimsy proof, followed by dogmatic sureness of their guilt. But for Aquinas, even unspoken suspicion was a vice. 'From the very fact that a man thinks evil of another without sufficient cause,' he wrote, 'he despises him unduly, and therefore does him an injury.' In Woolf's case, she voiced her doubts in essays, to friends in letters, though her most brutal slurs against Joyce were private. Her epistolary insults were what Aquinas called 'backbiting': tarnishing someone's name, but not publishing it.

In reading *Ulysses* this way, Virginia Woolf was certainly unfair to Joyce. But she was not wholly corrupt. Aristotle parcelled up injustice neatly into four kinds: misadventure, negligence, unjust act and unjust person. The least offensive is a simple mistake: someone has lost out, but unwittingly and unexpectedly so. Negligence arises from ignorance, but predictably: the guilty party should have known better. Crimes of passion, said Aristotle, include transgressions of conceit or rage. The consequences are straightforward, but we do not choose them rationally. 'When men do such harmful and mistaken acts they act unjustly,' Aristotle wrote, 'but this does not imply that the doers are ... wicked'. The truly depraved soul, he continued, is cold-blooded. She deliberately, and with full awareness of the implications, robs someone of their dues. Woolf was not cankered in this way. Hers was merely an unjust act. She was driven not by conscious cruelty, but by anger and pride—the arrogance of a talented but anxious artist, affronted by a commoner's audacity. This is what Aquinas, following Aristotle's lead, attributed to the irrational parts of the soul. 'When a man hates or despises another, or is angry with or envious of him,' wrote Aquinas, 'he is led by slight indications to think evil of him'. Struggling with her own burgeoning fiction, it took little for Woolf to see artistic vulgarity in Joyce's carnal, all too casual material.

RECTITUDE

In January 1941, James Joyce died in Zurich of a perforated ulcer. Woolf had written little of him over the decades since she first read *Ulysses*. In her diary, she reflected on the Irish author's age—they were almost exact contemporaries. There is a hint of coalition in her words, as if Woolf were looking back with less malice on a literary comrade. She recalled putting the book in a drawer because of its 'indecency', then pulling it out after a visit from Katherine Mansfield. But most poignantly, she described vividly the rapture and banality of its pages. 'I bought the blue paper book, & read it here one summer I think with spasms of wonder, of discovery,' she wrote, '& then again with long lapses of immense boredom.' The overtones of disgust and contempt were gone, replaced by a strange alloy of amazement and monotony. Woolf was silent about Joyce's failings, reflecting only upon her own considered response to the novel. Critics might demur on *Ulysses'* shortcomings, finding themselves enchanted not jaded—just as others might be inexplicably thrilled by every page of Wittgenstein or Proust. But if true, this simply means Woolf was hasty or too proud, not that she was unjust. Three months before her own death, Virginia Woolf regained the equanimity towards Joyce that fairness demanded. She turned a too-close rival into a safely distant collaborator.

Woolf did not have to worship Joyce to behave justly. She had to compensate for her creative anguish and high bourgeois imperiousness—a redemption achieved by time, not effort. But the decades only revealed what was already there: a generous concern for superior literature. Woolf was driven by an abiding desire for excellence in prose, composition, acuity—for all the splendour of her own oeuvre, she was also a fervent reader. Her reaction to Proust, for example, was meticulous but gushing. ('One has to put the book down and gasp,' she wrote to Roger Fry.) Behind her habitual fairness was first a devotion to the work; the willingness to give herself to the words, which she endorsed in 'How Should One Read a Book?' But justice also asked for a broader concern, not simply for particular novels or essays, but for their commonalities.

'Thus, with our taste to guide us,' she wrote, 'we shall venture beyond the particular book in search of qualities that group books together'. Reading gave not only gratification, but also standards.

In this, Woolf's was what Aquinas called a just will, controlled 'by the rectitude of the reason'. By the will, the theologian meant what he called 'rational appetite': a longing that can comprehend, and reflect upon, what it wants. He believed human beings are unique in this. Animals and plants have tendencies and impulses, but these are not fully logical. We can think, not only about means and ends, but also about why these ends are worthwhile; what higher goods they uphold or undo. The still-popular idea of the will as an invisible puppeteer, moving fancy and flesh, is dubious. But with a little generosity, Aquinas's concept is helpful. Justice is possible because the will is amenable to reflection; because, as readers, we can steer our slender yearnings with a yoke and a map.

This justice does not ask for a universal, eternal decree of excellence. As Aristotle noted, we sometimes need a lead ruler: a malleable notion of worth, which fits the specifics. This is how Virginia Woolf enriched her conception of literary goodness: 'a rule only lives when it is perpetually broken by contact with the books themselves'. To achieve this sensitivity to texts, we have to overcome our egocentrism or lust for easy generalisations. We grant our own thrills or ennui, arousal or revulsion, but we also try to make sense of the work's origins: the schools of thought, traditions of beauty, cultures of craft at work. If we hope to judge the author, we have to tease apart our quirks and hobbyhorses from theirs; our assumptions as against their intentions; our potential accomplishments versus their actual achievements. In Woolf's case, she had to distinguish between rightful frustration and malicious contempt for

Joyce; between existential threat and historical collaborator; between class markers and aesthetic flaws. While she failed to achieve this with *Ulysses*, her overall approach to texts was just. And Woolf's description of this movement, from experience to examination, speaks to her judicious taste:

> To continue reading without the book before you, to hold one shadow-shape against another, to have read widely enough and with enough understanding to make such comparisons alive and illuminating—that is difficult; it is still more difficult to press further and to say, 'Not only is the book of this sort, but it is of this value; here it fails; here it succeeds; this is bad; that is good'.

This is not to say that Woolf and Aquinas shared a conception of ultimate goodness, or even that the Christian theologian's neat divine finality is possible. Rather, this simple notion of justice makes sense of Woolf's orientation to the written word: a continually civilised palate, sporadically failed by lapses into conceit, fear and envy.

EXCELLENCE ENTIRE

There is another kind of reader's justice, which provides a broad literary ideal rather than a single kind of evenhandedness. In his *Nicomachean Ethics*, Aristotle noted that legislation pushes us to develop every virtue. A good citizen will not shirk duties, or assault peers, or avoid responsibility—she will show courage, temperance and pride. Aristotle's point was that, in order to live well in a community, we actually need all the excellences: dispositions that allow us to give others their dues on every occasion. 'Justice in this sense,' he wrote, 'is not part of excellence but excellence entire'.

Take *Ulysses* itself. To do justice to Joyce's masterwork, I need a swag of virtues. In episode eleven, Bloom narrates his meeting with an Irish republican. The hero describes the one-eyed caricature, sitting portentously with engraved seastones on his girdle—'tribal images of many Irish heroes and heroines of antiquity'. A list follows: over ninety figures, ranging from obvious Celtic legends like Conn of the Hundred Battles, to Dante, Mohammed and Beethoven. Without patience, it is easy to skip names, or allow the passage to blur—the point can be taken without noting every single line. But the hilarity of Joyce's chapter arises from the slow build-up of absurdity, and the way reasonableness is dotted with idiocy, plain-spoken fact with outrageous grandiosity. There is also a comedic rhythm to the passage, which reminds me of Stewart Lee's comedy: a humour of cadence as much as content. Read hurriedly, Joyce's wit is lost.

Ulysses is also an invitation to curiosity. What Woolf saw as schoolboy pretence can also be *about* schoolboy pretence. Witness the third episode, a stream-of-consciousness commentary by Stephen Dedalus. Stephen is something of a stand-in for Joyce himself, and in this 'Proteus' chapter the young man sprays his learning over the vellum. The first few pages alone reference Aristotle, Christian myth and theology, and German art criticism, and skip from English (in Joyce's lyrical mode) to German, French and Latin. This reveals not only the many sources of Joyce's education, but also the divide between his protagonist's learning and his anxiety. For all the bravado of his schooling, Stephen is thick with doubts and griefs. He mocks his own literary ambitions, and reveals his ambivalence about fatherhood; he has a careful mind for facts and theories, but is obsessed with the insubstantiality of things. And these themes are expressed *in* his academic references. Arianism taught the separateness of Holy Father and Son ('Where is poor dear Arius to try conclusions?'), but Stephen cannot seem to shake the presence of his dad. 'Wombed in sin darkness I was too, made not begotten,' Joyce writes. 'By them, the man with my voice and my eyes and a ghostwoman with ashes on her breath.' Read without some inkling of the universe of possibilities surrounding it, *Ulysses* loses its singular artistry.

The novel also asks for bravery, of a stripe. The penultimate chapter is a homecoming: Stephen Dedalus and Leopold Bloom arriving at the latter's home early in the morning. Like so much of *Ulysses*, it is written in a distinctive style: the catechism, in this case. Instead of poetic or journalistic prose, more familiar to highbrow or lowbrow readers (to use Woolf's own terms), Joyce deploys the abstract terminology of science and theology. I learn information about the novel itself—the ballast of facts that gives fiction credibility. But it is given with satirical precision. Near the beginning of the episode, Leopold, having forgotten his keys, vaults a wall and enters the kitchen by the scullery. Stephen, meanwhile, is still outside waiting:

What discrete succession of images did Stephen meanwhile perceive?

Reclined against the area railings he perceived through the transparent kitchen panes a man regulating a gasflame of 14 CP, a man lighting a candle, a man removing in turn each of his two boots, a man leaving the kitchen holding a candle of 1 CP.

These passages are funny but also shocking, as Joyce was undermining the traditional novel. Fiction is often defined by its verisimilitude—style that allows the audience to forget. Joyce refuses to identify with any one mode of prose, and constantly displays his craft. *Ulysses*, despite its unity of ideas, themes and structure, is a fragmented work, confronting the reader with varying impressions in varied languages. What makes *Ulysses* particularly impressive is that he achieves this while also offering a very human story. Still, it is not possible for me to read Joyce without a loss of trust in the straightforward verity of the canon. At the very least, Joyce's ambition is overwhelming: how to write after this? This is why TS Eliot, who recommended *Ulysses* to Woolf, was so adamant. 'The book would be a landmark,' he reportedly told her, 'because it destroyed the whole of the 19th Century'. If the novel fails to offer *Mrs Dalloway*'s psychological intricacy, it succeeds as an antidote to the disease of literary credulity. And in this, it asks for courage: the backbone to read and perhaps grieve for the illusions of the earnest bibliophile. To do justice to Joyce, I must be brave enough to recognise his needful damage.

While this is only one novel, the consequence is clear: the perfect reader cannot rest on a single excellence, but must cultivate as many as possible. Different works can ask for different virtues—Joyce might not test my temperance, while Woolf's gorgeous prose in 'On Re-Reading Novels' demands far less patience than the Victorian works she cites. But to read widely and with justice, we have to approach Aristotle's ideal. This will not be his *megalopsychos*, or great-souled man, whose stride is long and voice deep. It will be his less aloof literary doppelgänger: a reader who works ceaselessly to develop her many-sided merits.

ASPIRING TO DUES

The canonical hugeness of Woolf and Joyce gives justice an epic feel—as if evenhandedness were reserved for Olympians. But justice applies to all, by definition. Even if some authors deserve fewer plaudits, this is only because we have first given them their dues. And this applies to works we relish, as we can also be unjust with our adulation.

The stories of HP Lovecraft, for example, are classic pulp—tales that entertain with misanthropic creepiness. The prose is overblown, the surprises few and mild, and the mood monotonous. 'Then, in the middle of October,' he wrote in 'Cool Air', 'the horror of horrors came with stupefying suddenness.' Ironically, phrases like this achieve exactly the opposite of their content. Lovecraft's bigotry also ruins naïve enjoyment. His works, private and public, are soaked with disdain for other ethnicities and cultures, including African Americans, Jews and the 'bastard mess of stewing mongrel flesh without intellect' he saw in New York's Chinatown. He was also disgusted by sex and reproduction. Lovecraft was a vulgar Puritan, whose prose was a little more cultivated than his opinions. Doing justice to this man means recognising his ugly opinions, chronic alienation and limited finesse.

But it also means confronting Lovecraft's popularity. Millions of readers, without his chauvinism or estrangement, revel in his fiction. Despite his telling and not showing, his clumsy climaxes ('you see I died that time eighteen years ago'), his psychological narrowness, his fumbling imbalance between vagueness and detail—despite all this and more, there can sometimes be nothing more engrossing and strangely uplifting that an evening with Lovecraft's bleak New England. There is a genuine art to his tales, particularly his Cthulhu Mythos, which affords a mood of irredeemable aversion to life. It is unforgettable. The constantly florid phrasing evokes clammy resignation: the prose of men trying but failing to cope with forces beyond them. At the same time, Lovecraft makes the hideous seem ordinary. His phantasmagoria is that of a clerk, not a god or warrior prince. And perhaps most importantly, what he offers is not a study of human beings, but of their universe: a teeming, cruel, utterly foreign infinity. 'In Lovecraft,' wrote French novelist Michel Houellebecq, 'one does not meet any truly human specimens.' It is no injustice to Lovecraft to say that his interest was in the inexplicable jar, not the fragile, deluded specimens inside. As an author of short stories, he lacked the dignity and nuance of Hemingway or even Borges (who wrote a poor Lovecraft parody). But his fiction is, for what it is, literally dreadful.

Eric Van Lustbader has written many bestsellers, including *The Ninja*, which I read with credulity (and tumescence) as a teenager. His novels feature handsome protagonists with calloused fists and exotic sensibilities, international conspiracies, Asian martial arts magic and plenty of carnal metaphors. 'Her sex felt like a furnace as she guided him into her,' Lustbader wrote in *The Ninja*. 'She rammed her belly against him as he buried himself to the hilt'. Why put a working sword in a forge? Never mind: she was hot and he was deep. Lustbader's prose was rightly lambasted by several reviewers. 'Mr. Lustbader is especially fond of torture scenes,' wrote *The New York Times*, 'but the real torture lies in getting through his sentences.' The same newspaper wrote huffily that Lustbader's style displays 'the kind of flourishes prized by organizations that teach writing through the mail'. Reviewers also picked up on the novelist's orientalist fantasies: of ancient Asian mysticism, gender lore and combat prowess. Japanese women were like dangerous origami—challenges to be opened with 'infinite care and deliberateness', and 'filled with exquisite tenderness and devious violence'. In fact, Lustbader's female characters were often thin and brittle: personas without depth or dynamism. (Like Gelda, the abused lesbian sex worker, who uses a Remington revolver as a dildo.)

It is easy to trivialise Lustbader's achievements—the schlock phrasing and fetish concepts of mass paperback pulp. He is not a novelist of nuance or advanced scholarship. But as a teenager, *The Ninja* and its sequels were an introduction to a new prose style and philosophy. Lustbader refused flat journalistic phrasing, broke high school grammar rules (never begin a sentence with 'but'), and played freely with similes. 'There's nothing worse for me,' he wrote, 'than a storyteller without style.' Two decades after first reading *The Ninja*, I cannot say Lustbader's style impresses me. But his words were unusual—they seemed to take themselves seriously as performers. Lustbader also wrote long passages explaining Japanese ethics, politics, history and aesthetics—from the idea of 'face', to the Bushido code, to haiku poetry. While his analysis was simplistic, the novelist prompted me to think more carefully about culture and history. In this, Lustbader achieved his own ideal, that of publishing educational fiction. To do justice to the author, I have to overcome my backward cringe and confess: I came for the sex and violence, but stayed for the schooling.

CONFESSIONS AND CORRECTIONS

For the reader, justice is an aspiration, and a correction when this fails. Either way, it requires a willingness to take an author seriously, recognising their labour by committing to it sensitively and critically. This is always partial, since the writer is only envisioned behind—and often within—her work. This is true whether the author is an ancient fable like Homer, or a gabby festival panellist: we invent the author. This is no glib rejection of the author's reality. *All* relationships involve some speculation. We project 'inner lives' into others, making as many errors as we do about ourselves. Transparency is inhuman. Yet this does not stop us trying to comprehend and judge others' accomplishments—every day we speak easily of failure and conquest, contributing and undermining, master and novice. The same is true of text. The author deserves her dues, even if this means questioning her motives, or revealing the edges of her talent.

As beings and as readers, Aristotle's 'complete excellence' is rare. We can be hasty, petty and stuck-up. We can groan and curse works that are not written for us; that belong to audiences of another sensibility, maturity or mood. We can shred writers for our own distraction or depression. This is why justice as a specific virtue is crucial: it compensates for our other failings. Justice allows us to at least stop before we laud or blame with smug decisiveness. A just reader distinguishes between emotion and estimation; pauses between judgement and proclamation. She gives dues, not always by interpreting perfectly, but by admitting that dues are deserved and lacking. Yes, Woolf was unjust to Joyce, and nastily so. But a lasting kinship to justice prompted her confessions and corrections.

And, I hope, mine.

THE LUMBER ROOM

Sherlock Holmes was a bizarre man, but mundane in at least one way: he saw books chiefly as handy things. 'A man should keep his little brain-attic stocked with all the furniture that he is likely to use,' he said in 'The Five Orange Pips', 'and the rest he can put away in the lumber-room of his library, where he can get it if he wants it.' The lumber room was set aside in old estates to store tables, chairs, commodes—a storeroom of convenience.

For Holmes, reading was simply a technical skill for finding facts. He picked up the crime reports and agony aunt columns ('always instructive'), and that was all his forensic craft required. Here, the reader is purely a collector of obvious things, and the only doubt is deductive. Texts lose their signature anxiety, and become utilitarian mind furniture.

No doubt the written word can be straightforwardly useful: instruction manuals and digests, signs and plaques. But libraries are also constellations of wonder, reverie and shock. Conan Doyle's younger contemporary Saki echoed this point in his typically wry short story, 'The Lumber Room'. Set in a fictional seaside town, Jagborough, it has a young boy punished for his transgressions. Having dumped a frog in his bowl of bread and milk, Nicholas is left at home while his cousins head off for a beach visit. As his aunt tries foolishly to keep him from the gooseberry garden, Nicholas steals a key and lets himself into the mansion's locked lumber room. He finds a tapestry depicting a hunter, dogs and stag. Sitting on a roll of Indian hangings, Nicholas starts to daydream. Perhaps the hunter, crouching in long grasses, is a poor shot. But if so, how will be protect himself and his hounds from the wolves, prowling among the trees? Nicholas moves on, still hidden from his aunt. He discovers candlesticks, a teapot, a box of figurines, a book of exotic birds—'objects of delight and interest claiming his instant attention'.

The boy is never caught. And as the family sits to an awk-wardly silent tea, Nicholas too is quiet. 'It was just possible, he considered, that the huntsman would escape with his hounds,' wrote Saki, 'while the wolves feasted on the stricken stag.' The fantasy continues.

This is the thrill of pages: the discovery, often in child-hood, of things that incite invention; the hint of dangers pri-vately confronted, when one's family is far away; the fantasies that one chews on like a bone, while fidgeting with dinner.

To write about my library, which informed and inspired *The Art of Reading*, is to describe a lumber room much closer to Nicholas's than Sherlock's.

LIBERATING PAGES

Aesop's Fables is a compendium of dubious morality tales, which often tries to edify with agony and humiliation. My Collins (1951) edition, illustrated by Harry Rountree, has a huge, heavy font—perfect for the cumbersome messages of prudence.

The Book of the Thousand and One Night is pure adventure. Richard Burton's famous translation, considered pornography when first published, is still a marvel. If not for his fidelity to Arabic language and culture, then for his playfulness with English. My edition (Arthur Baker, 1953) also has atmospheric illustrations by WH Cuthill, which included the—to my childhood eyes—exotic kingdom of bare nipples.

While her prose and prejudices have dated, Enid Blyton's *The Magic Faraway Tree* remains awesome: branches that take unaccompanied children to unbelievable lands. Dorothy Wheeler's drawings, in my printing (George Newnes, 1947), still have a simple charm.

But they cannot compete with the whimsy of EH Shepard's sketches for *Winnie the Pooh* (Methuen & Co., 1946). The enchantment, verve and melancholy of AA Milne's series still get to me, particularly as I now have an Eeyore and Tigger of my own. (Thank you, Nikos and Sophia, for listening.) All these children's stories are available in many editions, new and second-hand—and often for free, digitally.

The same is true of Conan Doyle's tales. My edition of *The Celebrated Cases of Sherlock Holmes* (Octopus Books, 1986) still has its faux-gilt page edges and ersatz leather cover. But his works are available cheaply in all formats. While these detective tales cannot compete with the psychological nuance and forensic precision of modern crime stories, Sherlock

Holmes remains a singular hero—for his idiosyncrasies as much as for his genius. Doyle's style, a hundred years on, has much Watson to it: robust, reliable, a little huffy.

Vladimir Nabokov's *Speak, Memory* (Penguin, 2000) is thick with reflections—on memory, pre-revolution Russia, butterflies, exile, for example—and polished character portraits, all in his masterful prose.

Germaine Greer's recollection of literary hunger is from *The Pleasure of Reading* (Bloomsbury, 1992), edited by Antonia Fraser.

Maps and Legends (McSweeney's, 2008), by Michael Chabon, contains some typically thoughtful observations about pulp, comics and identity (especially Jewish). I have not quoted from his brilliant *The Amazing Adventures of Kavalier and Clay* (Fourth Estate, 2002), set in the United States during the golden age of superheroes. But it prompted me to seek out his ideas about popular culture—I was not let down. If my nods to Batman, Ghost Rider and Green Lantern leave you smiling or just curious, pick up Chabon's novel.

My first introduction to Orhan Pamuk was *My Name is Red* (Faber & Faber, 2011), a thrilling story set in Ottoman Turkey, often told from the perspective of things: a coin, a tree, a corpse. His essays on art, literature and life, *Other Colours* (Faber & Faber, 2007), lack the surreal luminosity of that novel, but include some fine discussions of his craft and divided world.

Alongside her culture and acumen, Edith Wharton was a brilliant prose stylist. Her *A Backward Glance* (Century, 1987) provides a glimpse of her life and era, but also provides paragraphs I can drink without becoming full. The same publisher has issued many of Wharton's works, and they are readily available second-hand.

My opinion of Jean-Jacques Rousseau is given in *Philosophy in the Garden* (Melbourne University Press, 2012). Suffice it to say that his *Confessions* (Penguin, 1953) is the timeless record of a modern mind revealing (and concealing) itself with talent.

Every issue of *The Paris Review* includes interviews with authors: from novelists, to playwrights, to biographers. For anyone interested in the genesis of literary nous, this magazine is a quarterly boon. The interview with William Gibson is in issue 197 (2011), but many other authors mentioned in *The Art of Reading* feature in archives. Dennis Nurkse's 'Learning to Read' is from 213 (2015). If subscription is too expensive, good public libraries will have current and back issues.

I have reservations about Jean-Paul Sartre's philosophy and personality, which I detail in *Philosophy in the Garden*. But his work on writing and reading is excellent. *What is Literature?* (Philosophical Library, 1949) is a bold account of literature's two freedoms, written in the same clear prose he celebrates. Sartre's *Words* (Hamish Hamilton, 1964) is a profound and strikingly written story of the philosopher's childhood and maturation. As with *Nausea*, this is Sartre at his best: fictionalising his own impressions.

I have my wife's paperback of Simone de Beauvoir's *Memoirs of a Dutiful Daughter* (Penguin, 1972), the first volume of her autobiography. Less grandiose but more moving than *Words*, *Memoirs* is also a rich record of pre-war France.

Herbert Marcuse's discussion of 'holiday reality' comes from *The Aesthetic Dimension* (Beacon Press, 1978)—still a striking defence of art's autonomy, and still available with its aesthetically challenging original cover of black, red and burnt orange.

Dickens's reflection is from *David Copperfield*, which drew heavily on his own childhood. Having worked in a second-hand bookshop for years, I can say with some weariness that Dickens is everywhere, and cheap.

Seamus Heaney's 'The Bookcase' is in his typically suggestive collection *Electric Light* (Faber & Faber, 2001). Look for the neon salmon cover.

The description of poetry snatching back the restless word comes from Hans-Georg Gadamer, 'Philosophy and Poetry', in *The Relevance of the Beautiful* (Cambridge University Press, 1996), edited by Robert Bernasconi.

My ideas of objects are echoed in Levi R Bryant's *The Democracy of Objects* (Open Humanities Press, 2011). Bryant is part of a growing philosophical trend—often called speculative realism—that tries to do justice to the universe beyond human consciousness, without lapsing into supernaturalism or naïve realism.

Marcel Proust's *On Reading* (Souvenir Press, 1971) is typically Proustian: books as repositories of the lost past. It is also, in this edition at least, a beautiful thing: mottled emerald and burgundy cloth.

Hannah Arendt only briefly discusses the written word, but *The Human Condition* (Doubleday Anchor, 1959) is a classic analysis of modern life, and the loss of freedom. My old paperback is held together by tape, but a revised edition by Chicago University Press (1998) is available.

Stoppard's quip is from *The Pleasure of Reading*.

On dementia and reading, studies include: Hui-Xin Wang, Anita Karp, Bengt Winblad and Laura Fratiglioni, 'Late-Life Engagement in Social and Leisure Activities Is Associated with a Decreased Risk of Dementia', *American Journal of Epidemiology*, Volume 155, Number 12 (2002); Joe Verghese, Richard B Lipton, Mindy J Katz, Charles B Hall, Carol A Derby, Gail Kuslansky, Anne Ambrose, Martin

Sliwinski and Herman Buschke, 'Leisure Activities and the Risk of Dementia in the Elderly', *New England Journal of Medicine*, Number 348 (2003); Anita Karp, Stéphanie Paillard-Borg, Hui-Xin Wang, Merrill Silverstein, Bengt Winblad and Laura Fratiglioni, 'Mental, Physical and Social Components in Leisure Activities Equally Contribute to Decrease Dementia Risk', *Dementia and Geriatric Cognitive Disorders*, Volume 21, Number 2 (2006). The last paper reports that different kinds of leisure—physical, social and intellectual—are more effective together than alone. A more cautious finding is from Hui-Xin Wang, Weili Xua and Jin-Jing Peib, 'Leisure Activities, Cognition and Dementia', *BBA Molecular Basis of Disease*, Volume 1822, Issue 3 (2012). This review of various studies concludes that research requires more standardisation and specificity. For example, the kind, intensity and duration of 'mental activity' (which includes reading) is not specified.

I discuss Haruki Murakami's excellent *What I Talk About When I Talk About Running* (Vintage, 2009) in *How to Think About Exercise* (Pan Macmillan, 2014).

Anne E Cunningham and Keith E Stanovich's 'What Reading Does For the Mind' is in *American Educator*, Volume 22 (1998). The research on brain connectivity is from 'Short- and Long-Term Effects of a Novel on Connectivity in the Brain', *Brain Connectivity*, Volume 3, Issue 6 (2013). The authors are Gregory S Berns, Kristina Blaine, Michael J Prietula, and Brandon E Pye. The work on theory of mind is from 'Reading Literary Fiction Improves Theory of Mind', *Science*, Volume 342, Number 6156 (2013), by David Comer Kidd and Emanuele Castano. The latter two studies are fascinating contributions to the science of reading, but the conclusions hyped by the popular media are dubious.

John Dewey's *Art as Experience* (Minton, Balch & Company, 1934) offers a theory of aesthetic experience without idealistic fantasies, fetishism of genius, or obscure jargon. My clothbound first edition is still in good nick, but newer copies are about.

My edition of Homer's *The Iliad* (The Folio Society, 1996), is what we called, in the second-hand bookshop, a 'jelly bean': embellished, expensive, a little pretentious. But Robert Fagles's visceral modern translation is marvellous. Grahame Baker Smith's stark illustrations add to the atmosphere of mythic immediacy. The same translation is also available in paperback, by Penguin. For a rhyming *Iliad*, Alexander Pope's stately eighteenth-century translation still sings.

Deborah Levy's psychologically astute novella *Swimming Home* (Faber & Faber, 2012) cut me into tiny pieces. Prose like industrial diamonds.

George Orwell's *Keep the Aspidistra Flying* (Penguin, 2010) lacks the polish and long view of *Nineteen Eighty-Four*, but as a portrait of literary hackery and *ressentiment* it is spot on.

Like his *Batman: Year One* (DC, 2005), Frank Miller's *The Dark Knight Returns* (DC, 2002) is a bleak but sophisticated graphic novel, which uses diverse prose and visual styles to tell the Batman story. While recent runs by writer Scott Snyder and artist Greg Capullo have deepened the Dark Knight mythos, Miller's work has lost none of its original power. Read him alongside anarchist Alan Moore to compensate for the former's fascist tendencies. Typical of its era, Ron Marz's *Green Lantern* #54 (1994) mistakes superficial brutality for psychological realism.

My *Nicomachean Ethics* is part of the two-volume *The Complete Works of Aristotle* (Princeton University Press, 1984), edited by Jonathan Barnes. Aristotle's discussion of *hexis* also appears in *On the Soul*. All Aristotle's lectures are available new, second-hand and as public domain downloads. The university editions often have more careful translations, as well as commentary. German philosopher Peter Sloterdijk has a brief but succinct discussion of *hexis* in *You Must Change Your Life* (Polity Press, 2013), in the chapter 'Habitus and Inertia'.

One of the finest modern interpreters of Aristotle is virtue theorist and communitarian Alasdair MacIntyre. *After Virtue* (Duckworth, 1984) made a massive and needful contribution to contemporary ethical debate. MacIntyre's essays, including those on the nature and value of ethical debate itself, are collected in *The Tasks of Philosophy* and *Ethics and Politics,* both published by Cambridge University Press (2006). His *A Short History of Ethics* (Routledge, 1998) is a succinct critical guide to the history of moral thought. His *Whose Justice? Which Rationality?* (University of Notre Dame Press, 1989) is an excellent guide to the different (and rival) traditions of justice.

Like those of MacIntyre, Gilbert Ryle's ideas have influenced generations of English-speaking philosophers. His post-war work *The Concept of Mind* (Penguin, 1973) remains a necessary correction to many psychological shibboleths. It has been reissued by Cambridge University Press.

Tim Parks's *Where I'm Reading From* (Harvill Secker, 2014) features his essay 'The Writer's Job', part of a collection of clear and sometimes provocative essays on literary craft, interpretation, criticism and the market.

Flannery O'Connor's reflections on literature, culture and religion are collected in *Mystery and Manners* (Faber & Faber, 2001), edited by Sally and Robert Fitzgerald.

The astonishing 'eight out of ten' finding is from The Jenkins Group's 'Most Americans Think They Have a Book in Them', (PR Newswire, 2002). The Pew study is

reported here: http://www.pewinternet.org/2014/01/16/
a-snapshot-of-reading-in-america-in-2013/.

Martial's lament is from the third book of his *Epigrams*,
Volume 1: Spectacles, Books 1–5 (Harvard University Press,
1994), edited by DR Shackleton Bailey. Juvenal's *The Sixteen
Satires* (Penguin, 2004) is a literary séance, bringing ordinary
Rome to life in vivid stanza after stanza. (Footnotes help fill
in the historical gaps.) The irony is that the author himself
remains behind: we know very little about Juvenal's life. There
are worse legacies. The *cacoethes scribendi* phrase comes from
the seventh satire.

In *Principles of Art* (Oxford University Press, 1938),
RG Collingwood offers a careful and sympathetic defence
of art, as opposed to craft. He highlights the role of art in
encouraging emotional honesty and comprehension. Despite
the narrowness of the theory, Collingwood's work on aesthetics still plays a role in today's debates.

'On Dilettantism', notes for a planned work by Goethe
and Schiller, is from *Essays on Art and Literature* (Princeton
University Press, 1986), edited by John Gearey.

The late neurologist Oliver Sacks is always clear, humane
and curious. *The Mind's Eye* (Picador, 2011) is no exception.

A History of Reading (Penguin, 1997), by Alberto
Manguel, is neither an academic record nor a straight memoir,
but a combination of scholarship, autobiography and literary
criticism. His devotion to the written word is obvious.

Being and Time (Basil Blackwell, 1989) by Martin
Heidegger is one of the most important philosophical works
of the twentieth century. I discuss Heidegger's ideas elsewhere, including in *Distraction* (Melbourne University Press,
2008). Put simply: his analysis of the structure of everyday

existence is a powerful response to narrowly rationalistic and individualistic portraits of humanity.

Michel Foucault's 'What is an Author?' is from *Aesthetics, Method, and Epistemology* (Penguin, 2000). Edited by James D Faubion, this is the second volume of Foucault's essential works, 1954–84. The same collection includes a fascinating essay on Jules Verne, 'Behind the Fable'. Roland Barthes's phrase is from his famous 'The Death of the Author', *Image, Music, Text* (Hill & Wang, 1978), selected by Stephen Heath.

Augustine's *On Christian Teaching* (Oxford University Press, 2008) is a careful and very clear attempt to provide *the* message of the Bible.

I nod to Derrida in passing, but his *On Grammatology* (Johns Hopkins University Press, 1976) was on my mind as I wrote *The Art of Reading*. Not because I have deployed his theory of writing, but because Derrida himself is a careful interpreter. Yes, he is iconoclastic and obscure. But to read Derrida is to observe reading itself: wary, picky, but also reverential. Derrida genuinely cares about the written word, and deserves recognition for this. This note is pinned in place of my brief Derridean reflections, cut from an earlier draft.

Literary critic Geordie Williamson's elegant phrase comes from his assessment of Clive James in *The Monthly*, April 2013.

'Criticism of Criticism of Criticism' appears in HL Mencken's *Prejudices* (Vintage, 1958). The title makes sense. Mencken was elitist, bigoted and anti-Semitic (though he urged support for Europe's Jewish refugees). He was also an excellent critic, a proud Nietzschean (his elitism was consistent), and a powerful writer. His aphoristic talents are on display throughout his essays. He also reminds sombre, shut-in readers to snigger every now and then—if only at themselves.

'One horse-laugh is worth ten thousand syllogisms. It is not only more effective; it is also vastly more intelligent.'

THE INFINITE LIBRARY

Borges is a miniaturist of immensity and infinity. A first encounter with his stories is a revelation. 'The Library of Babel' appears with most of Borges's most well-known tales in *Labyrinths* (Penguin, 1970), edited by Donald A Yates and James E Irby. Borges's essays and other nonfiction are collected in *The Total Library* (Penguin, 2001), edited by Eliot Weinberger. His quote on re-reading is from *Jorge Luis Borges: Conversations* (University of Mississippi Press, 1998), edited by Richard Burgin. The choice of Emily Dickinson occurred in conversation with Alastair Reid and John Coleman, recorded in *Borges at Eighty* (New Directions, 2013), edited by Willis Barnstone. Barnstone himself is a gifted poet and translator, and raconteur of generosity and charm.

Edwin Williamson's *Borges: A Life* (Viking, 2004) gives a detailed account of the author's family, culture and landscape. James Woodall's *Borges: A Life* (Basic Books, 2004) is simpler and less scholarly. Both devote a surprising number of pages to guesswork about Borges's love life. A more concise literary biography is Jason Wilson's *Jorge Luis Borges* (Reaktion Books, 2006). It sheds light on the author's Argentinian milieu, but has less of the romantic speculation. Manguel's reminiscences are from *A History of Reading*.

David Hume's *A Treatise of Human Nature* is arguably the most important English-language work of philosophy. Certainly, Hume's influence is lasting and broad. My edition (Dent, 1949) comes in two pocket-sized volumes, but Hume's works are available widely and cheaply. Translation is no issue. I discuss Hume's ideas briefly in *How to Think About Exercise*.

Novelist John Updike's critical essays are a pleasure to read, whether on Borges or otherwise. 'The Author as Librarian' is from *Picked-Up Pieces* (André Deutsch, 1975). The same is true of poet and critic Clive James. His reflections on Borges appear in *Cultural Amnesia* (Picador, 2012). Umberto Eco's 'Between La Mancha and Babel' is collected in *On Literature* (Vintage Books, 2006).

Ludwig Wittgenstein does not make things simple, and he has been lambasted for being an obscurist or obfuscator. But I always close *Philosophical Investigations* (Basil Blackwell, 1956) *thinking*. His observations and questions make the taken-for-granted—of language and conception, for example—suddenly seem weird. Not because he has offered me a rival theory, but because he has goaded me to reflect.

Heidegger's *Introduction to Metaphysics* (Yale University Press, 1997) is often provocative and sometimes maddening. As a study of Heidegger's thinking and manias, it is fascinating. Heidegger also discusses the Presocratics in *Four Seminars* (Indiana University Press, 2003) and *What is Philosophy?* (Vision, 1956). The second of these is, among other things, a short but punchy celebration of philosophical astonishment. 'My Way to Phenomenology' contains some of Heidegger's autobiographical reflections, and is collected in *Philosophical and Political Writings* (Continuum, 2003), edited by Manfred Stassen. The rural idyll pretending not to be a rural idyll is 'Why Do I Stay in the Provinces?', in the same volume.

The Presocratic Philosophers (Cambridge University Press, 1983), edited by GS Kirk, JE Raven and M Schofield, contains the basic Presocratic texts in Greek and English, alongside helpful commentary.

Richard Wolin's *The Politics of Being* (Columbia University Press, 1990) is a careful analysis of Heidegger's politics. Heidegger's remark on his interpretation of Kant is reported by Bernd Magnus in his foreword to *Nietzsche's Philosophy of the Eternal Recurrence of the Same* (University of California Press, 1997), by Karl Löwith. The 'secret king' is Hannah Arendt's description, in 'For Martin Heidegger's Eightieth Birthday', *Martin Heidegger and National Socialism* (Paragon House, 1990), edited by Günther Neske and Emil Kettering. Hans-Georg Gadamer reflects on Heidegger's political failure in 'The Political Incompetence of Philosophy', in *The Heidegger Case* (Temple University Press, 1992), edited by Tom Rockmore and Joseph Margolis.

Zadie Smith's typically polished writings on writing (and reading) are collected in *Changing My Mind* (Penguin, 2009).

Mikhail Bakhtin writes about speech genres in *Speech Genres and Other Late Essays* (University of Texas Press, 1986), edited by Caryl Emerson and Michael Holquist. Emerson also edited Bakhtin's *Problems of Dostoyevsky's Poetics* (Manchester University Press, 1984), which is a brilliant analysis of the Russian novelist and the novel itself.

Pierre Bourdieu's work spotlights the social ground beneath philosophical leaps. *Pascalian Meditations* (Polity Press, 2000) is no exception.

Batman: A Death in the Family (DC, 2011), originally published over four issues from 1988 to 1989, was a pivotal point in modern superhero history. Not simply because it added new trauma to Batman's psychodrama, but because fans voted to let Robin, Jason Todd, live or die. (They chose well.) Writer Jim Starlin provides a thrilling, sometimes moving story, and Jim Aparo's pencils move easily between action and pathos. Adrienne Roy's colours (rendered before computerised colouring took over) are particularly vibrant. Philosopher Slavoj Žižek writes perceptively about Christopher Nolan's Batman films in *Trouble in Paradise* (Penguin, 2014).

BOREDOM AT BUCKINGHAM PALACE

The Uncommon Reader (Faber & Faber, 2007) by Alan Bennett is a quietly brilliant novella. Class, Englishness, regret, love and the liberating power of literature—Bennett folds a great deal into this paper plane. Bennett's reflections on these themes and more can be found in *Untold Stories* (Faber & Faber, 2005).

Readers of *Distraction* will know of my esteem for Henry and William James—apart and together. The novelist and the philosopher are a peevish but suggestive pairing. Most of their well-known works are available for free, and Henry's novels and short stories still stock retail classics shelves in cheap paperback editions. My *Golden Bowl* (Bodley Head, 1971) is from the eleven-volume collection, with introductions by James's biographer Leon Edel. But Ruth, my wife, recently picked up a beautiful two-volume *The Golden Bowl* (Macmillan, 1923) second-hand: the font is clearer, the volumes lighter, bound in handsome blue balloon cloth with art nouveau decorations on the cover and spine. An invitation to re-read. My *The Portrait of a Lady* (Oxford University Press, 1958) is octavo (so portable), and has an excellent introduction by Graham Greene. *The Complete Tales of Henry James* (Rupert Hart-Davis, 1962–64), edited by Leon Edel, cost half a week's rent. An extravagance I stand by, years later. William James's *Psychology: The Briefer Course* (University of Notre Dame Press, 1985) is very readable, and still illuminating.

Familiarity with Plato helps to make sense of Western civilisation, but he can also be read for pleasure. The Athenian was philosophically profound and artistically gifted—some of his dialogues are literary masterworks. My *Republic* is from *The Collected Dialogues* (Princeton University Press, 1961), edited by Edith Hamilton and Huntington Cairns. But there are countless translations in paperback, hardback (like the handsome dual language Loeb editions) and digital archive. Next to Plato, Aquinas seems plodding. But his *Summa Theologica* is precise, dogged and often wise—it is dogma, but not doctrinaire. My edition is a digital copy of the Benziger Brothers (1948) five-volume set. All references to Aquinas are from these volumes. Augustine's 'On Patience' is from *Nicene and Post-Nicene Fathers: First Series*, Volume III (Cosimo, 2007), edited by Philip Schaff.

De Inventione was Cicero's oratory handbook, written when he was young. He covers the virtues within a more general discussion about rhetoric. This is from *De Inventione, De Optimo Genere Oratorum, Topica* (William Heinemann, 1976), from the 28-volume dual language edition.

Dante's *Paradiso* (Anchor Books, 2007) is, for me, the least moving work of *The Divine Comedy*. But I was drawn to its exultant strangeness; the geometry and moral high-mindedness of Dante's ascent. This edition, translated by Robert and Jean Hollander, has the Italian on facing pages—it gave me at least a hint of the original's poetic rhythms. I also have a pocket edition by Oxford University Press (1951), which offers a more dated but less staid rhyming translation.

Herman Melville's *Moby-Dick* (Penguin, 1978) is one of the most extraordinary novels in English. Manners, mania, marine biology, maritime lore, moral philoso-phy, literature itself—this masterwork contains multitudes, including a gripping narrative of vengeance and memorable character studies.

Flashpoint (DC, 2011) by Geoff Johns, illustrated by Andy Kubert, is no great American novel. But its portrayal of a broken Thomas Wayne (Bruce's father) is excellent, and the final, silent moments with Bruce are perfect.

Delia Falconer's observation is from "'This Stuff Tastes of Window": Reading as a Writer', in *The Simple Act of Reading* (Vintage Books, 2015), edited by Debra Adelaide.

Dan Brown's *The Da Vinci Code* (Transworld, 2009) is not 'a quest almost as old as time itself', as the blurb promises. But it did prompt me to notice time passing.

Evelyn Waugh's moment of Jamesian joy comes from *The Diaries of Evelyn Waugh* (Penguin, 1984), edited by Michael Davie. It stands out amid the snark.

'Random Ageist Verses' by Peter Porter was published in *The Guardian*, 24 April 2010. It was part of a series on ageing, commissioned by Carol Ann Duffy.

THE NINJA OF UNFINISHEDNESS

Avenger! (Berkley Books, 1988) is part of a 6-volume set by Mark Smith and Jamie Thomson, originally published in the United Kingdom by Knight Books (1985). The disclaimer, that trying the featured techniques 'could lead to serious injury or death to an untrained user', was an instant recommendation. The English covers by Bob Harvey are superior, and I regret selling my copies.

The Sense of an Ending (Oxford University Press, 2000) is rightly considered a modern classic. Frank Kermode is of the finest English-speaking literary critics. He combines erudition and intellectual boldness with limpid prose. He also knows his way around an offhand joke: 'a reading of Proust is never repetitive because on each reading one skips different passages'. This is from 'Forgetting', in *Pieces of My Mind* (Farrar, Straus & Giroux, 2003).

Alfred North Whitehead's *Modes of Thought* (Macmillan, 1958) is a typically concise account of the tension, in science and philosophy, between precision, certainty and stasis on the one hand, and vagueness, doubt and dynamism on the other. Whitehead also reveals the importance of importance: it is a fact that not all facts matter.

Alan Moore's *Watchmen* (DC, 2014), illustrated by Dave Gibbons, is a masterful graphic novel. It offers a thrilling superhero story that simultaneously picks apart the conceits of the genre. It also includes careful character studies and pessimistic reflections on Realpolitik: perhaps the murder of honesty (literally and figuratively) is the price of peace.

'The Pursuit of the Ideal' is from *The Proper Study of Mankind* (Pimlico, 1998), edited by Henry Hardy and Roger Hausheer. Berlin is one of the most clear and charismatic voices of modern liberalism.

There is little information about Pseudo-Dionysius the Areopagite, though his *On the Divine Names and the Mystical Theology* (Amazon, 2010) is definitely Neo-Platonic, and probably from the fifth century. While Pseudo-Dionysius is writing fifteen hundred years before Heidegger, the mood of his treatise is sometimes less like that of traditional theology, and more like that of the German philosopher's late work: a refusal of metaphysical certainty. (But Dionysius has a bob each way.)

I write about Alexander Pope in *Philosophy in the Garden*: the poet's humour, charm and immense influence on literate England (including Jane Austen). His quip on wit comes from 'An Essay on Criticism', in *Collected Poems* (Dent, 1969).

JH Prynne's 'Moon Poem' is collected in *Poems* (Bloodaxe Books, 2015). His remark on authorship was reported by Robert Potts in *The Guardian*, 10 April 2004.

Leonard Woolf, the husband of Virginia, was a writer of rare candour and boldness. *Sowing* (The Hogarth Press, 1961) is part of a 5-volume autobiography, which provides a unique account of his era, life, marriage and career.

Ghost Rider #5 (1990), written by Howard Mackie and pencilled by Mark Texeira, is angsty pulp. While it has more subtlety than I realised (or wanted), it still suffers from 1990s excess: of simplistic violence, boilerplate prose and hair. The illustrations are vivid and dynamic.

I discuss TS Eliot's life and worldview in *Distraction*, particularly the relationship between religion, labour and poetry. Eliot exemplified an austerity and discipline that were alien to me as a teenager, but now make much sense. 'The Love Song of J Alfred Prufrock' is ubiquitous in collections and online. Mine is from *Collected Poems: 1909–1962* (Faber & Faber, 1970).

I read a pile of Clive Barker's novels in my early teens, including *Weaveworld* (Harper Collins, 1987). I revelled in the pacing and imagery, but remember nothing of the plots.

AS Byatt's *Still Life* (Vintage, 1995) is characteristically lyrical and brutal. I gave up after the death of the young mother—it was too soon after the grave illness of my wife. I will finish it.

Charlotte Wood's *Animal People* (Allen & Unwin, 2011) portrays the banal, comic awfulness of one man's malaise. Wood is faithful to modern Sydney's ambiance, and the creaturely fragility of human love.

Knowing how well Sartre can write, *Being and Nothingness* (Philosophical Library, 1956) is a colossal let-down—the prose is muck. But Sartre's defence of freedom, however falsely pure, is stirring. And his introspective passages are usually excellent.

GOSPEL UNTRUTHS

Kazantzakis's letters come from *Nikos Kazantzakis: A Biography Based on His Letters* (Bruno Cassirer, 1968), edited by his wife Eleni. This is not a traditional biography, but it does give a vivid portrait of the author's personality and style. *The Last Temptation* (Bruno Cassirer, 1960) remains a sophisticated and affecting portrait of the Christ. Mine is the first edition, with a striking cover illustration of a crucified hand by Walter Ritchie. But the new paperback editions by Simon & Schuster are affordable and well formatted.

Lewis Owens's interview with Rowan Williams, courtesy of Cambridge University, is available here: https://www.youtube.com/watch?v=Iz3JtpMMUxc. On the strife Kazantzakis's works caused in his homeland, see Michael Antonakes's 'Christ, Kazantzakis, and Controversy in Greece', in *God's Struggler* (Mercer University Press, 1996), edited by Darren JN Middleton and Peter Bien. On his relation to Greek orthodoxy, see 'Nikos Kazantzakis: Orthodox or Heterodox?', by Demetrios J Constantelos, in the same collection.

Ignatius of Antioch's statement of humility comes from his letter to the Trallians, in *Early Christian Writings: The Apostolic Fathers* (Penguin, 1987), edited by Andrew Louth.

To pick up Blaise Pascal's *Pensées* (Penguin, 1968) is to enter a second universe, characterised by equally intense vacancy and grace. Reason is rarely turned against itself with such brilliant brutality. Donald Adamson's *Blaise Pascal* (St Martin's Press, 1995) is a careful analysis of Pascal's work, which deftly combines his religious and scientific labours. The chapters on *Pensées* in John R Cole's *Pascal: The Man and His Two Loves* (New York University Press, 1995) offer a close analysis of Pascal's psychology. A more breezy (and sometimes hasty) biography is *Pascal's Wager* (Harper Collins, 2009) by James A Connor.

Friedrich Nietzsche's late notebooks edited by Rüdiger Bittner (Cambridge University Press, 2003) are essential for Nietzsche scholars. They are also packed with quips, revelations and explosive take-downs of European ideals. Still eye-opening.

Alfred North Whitehead's *Adventures of Ideas* (Cambridge University Press, 1933) is both a history of Western civilisation and an argument for what civilisation is, and requires. 'No fact is merely itself' comes from his *Modes of Thought*. Whitehead's 'Universities and Their Function' is from *The Aims of Education* (The Free Press, 1967). He argued for a reciprocity between research and teaching, lecturers and students, and between the faculties themselves—a vision of education that emphasises curiosity and imagination, without giving up on precise, rigorous reflection. Not, in other words, what is happening across the English-speaking world: managerial harassment, professional solipsism, and the transformation of universities into high-priced, low-quality credential factories. 'Education and Self-Education' comes from *Science and Philosophy* (Littlefield, Adams & Company, 1964).

Michael Moorcock's pinpricks at Tolkien's balloons occur in *Wizardry and Wild Romance* (Victor Gollancz, 1987). Tim Parks recommended making notes in 'Weapons For Readers', *New York Review of Books*, 3 December 2014.

Italo Calvino is a provocative (sometimes puckish) novelist and fascinating scholar of literature. His comment on the classics is from 'Why Read the Classics?', in *The Uses of Literature* (Harcourt, Brace and Company, 1986).

On my shelves are some excellent studies of Aristotle, Plato, Greek drama and human susceptibility—by thinkers like Alasdair MacIntyre, Iris Murdoch, Pierre Vidal-Naquet and John Gray. Martha Nussbaum's *The Fragility of Goodness* (Cambridge University Press, 1989) combines all of these fields, in an exceptional work of scholarship, reflection and prose.

My wife's copy of de Beauvoir's *The Second Sex* (Penguin, 1972) is falling apart, but many of the ideas hang together well. As a warning against naturalising social forces, it is eloquent and bold.

Peter Bien's comment on Kazantzakis and women is from the appendix of his scrupulous *Kazantzakis: Politics of the Spirit* (Princeton University Press, 2007).

APPETITE FOR DISTRACTION

The Red King (Pocket Books, 2005) by Andy Mangels and Michael A Martin kept me busy. As did David Mack's *Destiny* (Pocket Books, 2012). But Mack's 3-volume saga is far more ambitious: in breadth of storytelling and psychological detail.

For classic science fiction that takes more profound risks with form or substance, try John Brunner's *Stand on Zanzibar* (Arrow Books, 1971) or Brian Aldiss's *The Dark Light Years* (New English Library, 1971). Both are easy to find second-hand.

Iris Murdoch's 'The Sovereignty of Good Over Other Concepts' is collected in *The Sovereignty of Good* (Routledge, 2007). *Metaphysics as a Guide to Morals* is published by Penguin (1993). Some of Murdoch's Platonic sympathies are alien, but I am always challenged and informed by her arguments.

The same is true of AJ Ayer's logical positivism. His *Language, Truth and Logic* (Penguin, 2001) is bracing, and this recent edition has a neat introduction by Ben Rogers.

Mrs Dalloway (Oxford University Press, 2001) by Virginia Woolf is one of my favourite novels. It changed the way I think about literature, sanity and sociability. And the prose itself is stunning.

Larkin's 'The Old Fools' appears in *High Windows* (Faber & Faber, 1974).

My *Northanger Abbey* (Collector's Library, 2004) is part of a 6-volume set of small hardbacks, with (too) cute drawings by Hugh Thomson. Editions abound. Catherine Morland's story is the Austen novel I am drawn to least. Satire of a very specific literary style and personality, *Northanger Abbey* lacks the verve of *Pride and Prejudice* and the ethical and psychological subtlety of *Mansfield Park* and *Persuasion*.

F Scott Fitzgerald's 'The Crack-Up' is collected in an anthology of the same name (Penguin, 1974).

Like his *The World as Will and Idea* (Dent, 2002), Schopenhauer's 'On Books and Reading' can be found digitally for free, or collected in a number of new and second-hand volumes. Mine is from *Complete Essays of Schopenhauer* (Crown Publishers, 1932), which also contains 'On Thinking For Oneself'. This edition has a clumsy contents page and no index—a searchable digital version is more useful. Rüdiger Safranski's *Schopenhauer and the Wild Years of Philosophy* (Weidenfeld & Nicolson, 1989) is philosophically astute and elegantly written.

Most of Nietzsche's works are available in Penguin editions, but the Cambridge University Press (1995) *Human, All Too Human* includes a second volume of maxims, opinions and 'The Wanderer and His Shadow'. My *The Gay Science* is Kaufmann's Vintage (1974) edition. RJ Hollingdale's *Nietzsche: The Man and His Philosophy* (Routledge & Kegan Paul, 1965) is a sympathetic introduction to the philosopher's life and thought. In 'Nietzsche's Reading and Private Library, 1885–1889', Thomas Brobjer discusses Nietzsche's collection and habits, and argues persuasively for the importance of this study. The essay is from the *Journal of the History of Ideas*, Volume 58, Number 4 (1997). I discuss Nietzsche's *Gedankenbaum* in *Philosophy in the Garden*.

Roberto Calasso is an institution: Italian publisher, man of letters, polylingual scholar of myth and literature. His *Ardor* (Penguin, 2015) is a dizzying analysis of ancient Indian ritual, cosmology, ethics and philosophy. A revelation of analogical thinking.

NO I SAID NO I WON'T NO

Earlier I praised Virginia Woolf's *Mrs Dalloway*. Now is the moment to laud her essays, letters and diary: works of unfailingly fascinating prose. If I had to choose between her fiction and nonfiction, I would probably inch towards the latter. (And often have.)

Virginia Woolf's 'sacred fluid' comes from 'Old Bloomsbury', in *A Bloomsbury Group Reader* (Basic Blackwell, 1993), edited by SP Rosenbaum. The *Vogue* diary entry is from 6 May 1926 in *The Diary of Virginia Woolf*, Volume 3: 1925–30 (Penguin, 1983), edited by Anne Oliver Bell. The 'queasy undergraduate' description of Joyce is from 16 August 1922 in *The Diary of Virginia Woolf*, Volume 2: 1920–24 (Penguin, 1981), also edited by Bell. 'Modern Fiction', 'How Should One Read a Book?', 'Hours in a Library', 'The Leaning Tower' and 'On Re-Reading Novels' are from Virginia Woolf,

Collected Essays: II (Chatto & Windus, 1972), edited by Leonard Woolf. The letter to Roger Fry is 3 October 1922 in *The Letters of Virginia Woolf*, Volume 2: 1912–22 (Harcourt Brace Jovanovich, 1972), edited by Nigel Nicolson and Joanne Trautmann. 'Mr Bennett and Mrs Brown' is collected in Virginia Woolf, *Collected Essays: I* (Chatto & Windus, 1966), also edited by her husband. Woolf's protest to McCarthy is from 2 February 1941 in *The Letters of Virginia Woolf*, Volume 6: 1936–41 (Harcourt Brace Jovanovich, 1980) edited by Nigel Nicolson and Joanne Trautmann.

Leonard Woolf's *Beginning Again* (The Hogarth Press, 1964) is the third volume of his excellent memoirs. *Virginia Woolf* (Chatto & Windus, 1993) by Hermione Lee is a generous account of Woolf's life. Lee has a particularly revealing chapter devoted to Woolf's reading. See also James King's shorter *Virginia Woolf* (Penguin, 1995), on the relationship between Woolf's work and life.

Woolf's whine about servants is from 29 January 1918 in *The Letters of Virginia Woolf*, Volume 2: 1912–22. Her bigoted question about the lower classes is from 14 August 1918, *The Letters of Virginia Woolf*, Volume 1: 1888–1912 (Harcourt Brace Jovanovich, 1977), edited by Nigel Nicolson and Joanne Trautmann. Her confession of having her 'back up' is from 7 September 1922, *The Letters of Virginia Woolf*, Volume 2: 1912–22. She admitted to having 'scamped' its virtue the previous day.

Woolf's 'dead cat' comment is from 3 November 1936 in *The Diary of Virginia Woolf*, Volume 5: 1936–41 (Penguin, 1985), edited by Bell. The same volume contains Woolf's final recollection of Joyce, on 15 January 1941.

My edition of James Joyce's *Ulysses* (Bodley Head, 1960) is a squat, Brunswick green hardback—identical to my father's (whose edition I first borrowed). TS Eliot's opinion of Joyce is reported by Woolf, 26 September 1922, in *The Diary of Virginia Woolf*, Volume 2: 1920–24.

An example of Stewart Lee's comedy: https://www. youtube.com/watch?v=QQsknEsgz7s.

HP Lovecraft's tales are collected in *The Call of Cthulhu and Other Weird Stories* (Penguin, 1999), edited by ST Joshi. His racist comments are detailed in L Sprague de Camp's *Lovecraft: A Biography* (Hachette, 2011). A short but animated defence of Lovecraft's achievements is *H.P. Lovecraft: Against the World, Against Life* (Weidenfeld & Nicolson, 2006) by novelist Michel Houellebecq.

My old paperback of Eric Van Lustbader's *The Ninja* did not survive my undergraduate years. I replaced it recently with a very cheap digital edition, by Head of Zeus (2014). The first *New York Times* review is by Jack Sullivan, 10 April 1983. The second is by Peter Andrews, 7 June 1981. Lustbader's comment on style is from his website.

THE LUMBER ROOM

'The Lumber Room' is from *The Collected Short Stories of Saki* (Wordsworth, 1999), by Hector Hugh Munro (Saki was his pen name). Many are available digitally, for free. Despite his influence on writers like PG Wodehouse and AA Milne, Saki is less read today. His patience with children and animals, and refusal to suffer adult hypocrisy, are not dated at all.

ACKNOWLEDGEMENTS

Thanks to Philip Gwyn-Jones at Scribe UK for his support and zeal, and to Molly Slight and Sarah Braybrooke for their artful spruiking. Thanks also to designer Allison Colpoys for this elegant cover. Sally Heath was my original commissioning editor at MUP—I'm grateful for her enthusiasm, ear for tone, and wariness of prose tics.

I'm grateful to Sharon Galant and Benython Oldfield, my agents at Zeitgeist Media Group Literary Agency, who championed my work once again.

These authors were generous in conversation: Willis Barnstone, James Bradley, Delia Falconer, Robert Dessaix, Rebecca Giggs, Matt Lamb, Diane Setterfield and Geordie Williamson. Alison Croggon, Melissa Harrison, David Lebedoff and Gerard Wood read draft chapters. Thanks, all.

Michael Antonakes, with the help of Peter Bien, kindly sent his paper on Kazantzakis's controversies.

I'm grateful to my parents, Allana and David, for introducing me to the written word. Ruth Quibell is my partner in reading, writing and whatever falls between. Thank you for this rare project of twoness.